Genealogy in Ontario:
Searching the Records

Brenda Dougall Merriman
B.A., C.G.R.S.

THE ONTARIO HISTORICAL SOCIETY

Inner Cover maps by Fred Hill

ontario genealogical
society

This book was published with the assistance of the Ontario Ministry of Citizenship and Culture

Canadian Cataloguing in Publication Data

Merriman, Brenda Dougall
    Genealogy in Ontario: searching the records

Bibliography: p.
ISBN 0-920036-16-3.

1. Ontario – Genealogy. I. Ontario Genealogical Society. II. Title.

CS88.O58M47   1985   929'.3713   C85-093310-X

(front cover) Land petition of Margarite Grant, spinster, 1806. (PAC, RG 1 L3, Vol. 204A, Petition G8/4)

ISBN 0-920036-16-3

Printed in Canada

PREFACE

The popularity of genealogy and family history research has increased tremendously in Ontario as elsewhere in the past few years, particularly stimulated by our Canadian Centennial year in 1967, and by the Ontario Bicentennial in 1984. The number of genealogical requests now being received by public and private institutions has risen dramatically.

Despite this growth in interest, only brief guides to genealogical sources for tracing Ontario families have yet been available, and no comprehensive handbook has been published. The vast size of our province and its many excellent record groups have made it difficult to produce more than regional or local guides. This publication is designed to help meet that deficiency by providing an overview of basic resources.

Each ancestor hunter begins with different information, a different starting point, or eventually meets different problems. Therefore this book does not give you a step-by-step lesson nor might it answer every question that could arise in your research. Throughout the text we will refer to books, articles, and manuals which we feel are essential to good research (see full listings in Appendix II). We recommend that this book *Genealogy in Ontario: Searching the Records* be used in conjunction with another OGS publication, *Some Ontario References and Sources for the Family Historian*, as the latter contains an excellent bibliographic guide.

This particular book will deal with sources in our two largest repositories, the Public Archives of Canada (PAC) and the Archives of Ontario (AO). We hope to show where the records are, information needed to use them, their genealogical value, and some limitations or drawbacks associated with finding and using them.

Readers who pursue their searches in archives, museums, and libraries are advised to allow enough time to become familiar with each system and to learn locations of material sought.

BDM

ACKNOWLEDGMENTS

The author takes responsibility for any errors that may have crept into the text. However, the writing and editing of this book would not have been possible without the expertise and advice of certain individuals, either as recent consultants or as personal supporters over the years. My special thanks to the following:

At the Archives of Ontario:
    John Mezaks
    Richard Ramsey
    June Gibson
    Catherine Shepard

At the Public Archives of Canada:
    Patricia Kennedy

In the Ontario Genealogical Society:
    Bruce Elliott
    Marie Charbonneau
    Jim Kennedy
    George Hancocks
    Elizabeth Hancocks
    Norman Crowder

Joe Goski

My first tutor, Dennis Beardmore

TABLE OF CONTENTS

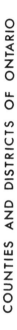

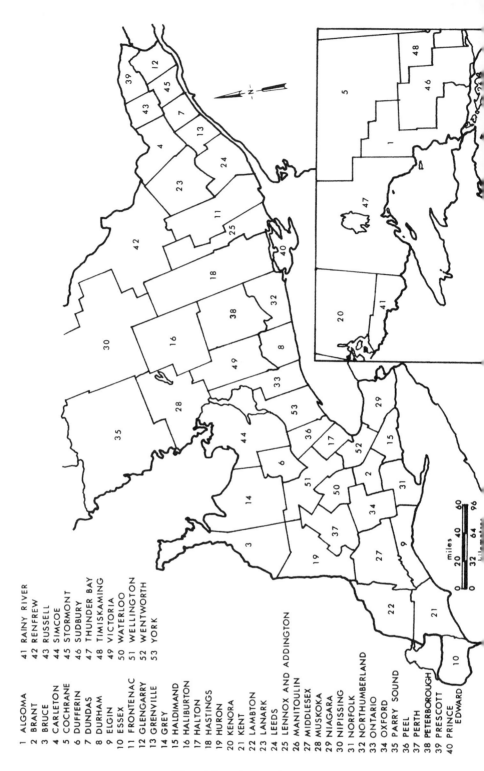

1 ALGOMA
2 BRANT
3 BRUCE
4 CARLETON
5 COCHRANE
6 DUFFERIN
7 DUNDAS
8 DURHAM
9 ELGIN
10 ESSEX
11 FRONTENAC
12 GLENGARRY
13 GRENVILLE
14 GREY
15 HALDIMAND
16 HALIBURTON
17 HALTON
18 HASTINGS
19 HURON
20 KENORA
21 KENT
22 LAMBTON
23 LANARK
24 LEEDS
25 LENNOX AND ADDINGTON
26 MANITOULIN
27 MIDDLESEX
28 MUSKOKA
29 NIAGARA
30 NIPISSING
31 NORFOLK
32 NORTHUMBERLAND
33 ONTARIO
34 OXFORD
35 PARRY SOUND
36 PEEL
37 PERTH
38 PETERBOROUGH
39 PRESCOTT
40 PRINCE EDWARD
41 RAINY RIVER
42 RENFREW
43 RUSSELL
44 SIMCOE
45 STORMONT
46 SUDBURY
47 THUNDER BAY
48 TIMISKAMING
49 VICTORIA
50 WATERLOO
51 WELLINGTON
52 WENTWORTH
53 YORK

Map of Ontario Counties.

INTRODUCTION

Hints for the Beginning Genealogist

GROUP CONTACT

For personal contact and do-it-yourself approaches, you should investigate joining a local genealogical society and the offering of genealogical research courses. Courses are sometimes run as evening classes or one-day weekend seminars by such groups as genealogical or historical societies, libraries, museums, archives, community colleges, or through a "continuing education" programme at local high schools and universities.

STUDY

The beginner's first step, collecting family information from home and relatives, is well-described in dozens of reference books which should be available at your local library. One example is *Searching For Your Ancestors* by Gilbert Doane. (See full listings of all books in Appendix II).

Procedures and methods for research may also be found in many books. We recommend *Genealogical Research Methods and Sources, Vol 1*, edited by Milton Rubincam, or Stevenson's *Search and Research*.

Already suggested as companion reading to this book is *Some Ontario References and Sources for the Family Historian*. Other recommended publications are *Readings in Ontario Genealogical Sources* edited by Don Wilson, and *The Canadian Genealogical Handbook* by Eric Jonasson.

SETTLEMENT OF ONTARIO

Settlement in Ontario by non-native peoples was initiated in an organized political way in 1783, although French fur traders, missionaries, and scattered settlers had established earlier communities. It was the arrival of Loyalists and disbanded King's soldiers that really forced the British to open "new" territory.

We would also suggest, as background reading, a succinct history of Ontario. *Upper Canada: The Formative Years, 1783-1841* by Gerald Craig is one example. Depending on the location and time period of your ancestors, you may find more interest in a local history (see Aitken's *Bibliography*, and ask for catalogues from publishers in Appendix II).

MAPS

One should always bear in mind that settlement grew along transportation routes, i.e. river and lake access, and later canals, roads, and railways. Thus it was along the Great Lakes water route and the rivers feeding it, that population first grew and spread out. Using a map with this knowledge often helps to follow movements of the next generation.

By all means try to obtain a map, preferably of pre-1968 vintage before Regional government led to several changes in place-names (see Appendix II).

As the population grew, the boundaries and jurisdictions of government changed from time to time. This will affect the location of certain records. The *township*, divided into concessions and then into lots, was the basic unit for land surveying. In *Families*, Vol. 15, No. 4 (1976), Eldon Weber writes on "Some Unusual Aspects of Early Land Surveys in Old Ontario".

Townships remained relatively unchanged up until 1968 in most areas. We strongly recommend "The Districts and Counties of Southern Ontario, 1777-1979, Two Centuries of Evolution" by Eric Jonasson in *Families*, Vol. 20, No. 2 (1981).

DISCOVERING
RESIDENTIAL
LOCATIONS

Problems with Places

After collecting all the information available from family members, your next goal is to find the ancestral *location* in Ontario if a specific reference has not yet turned up. We have already mentioned the importance of location in order to get at the appropriate records. What can you do if your only reference is to "Upper Canada" or "English Canada" or "Canada West", all used to indicate early Ontario? For the sake of consistency, we're going to call it *Ontario* throughout this text.

There are a few useful indexes that might help with this most basic problem, indexes that apply to the province as a whole:

Computerized Land Records Index
Index to Upper Canada Land Petitions
Index to Surrogate Clerk's Application Registers
(all described in later chapters)

Reid's *The Loyalists in Ontario*
Reid's *Marriage Notices of Ontario*
Wilson's *Ontario Marriage Notices*
Reid's *Death Notices of Ontario*
McKenzie's *Death Notices From the Christian Guardian 1836-1850*
The Ontario Register, now into Vol. 7

Even if you don't find a direct ancestor in these sources, you should be able to recognize groupings of the surname in certain areas, which is at least a starting point. When the Index to the 1871 Census has been completed, it will provide the most comprehensive source for regionalizing surnames.

There are many Ontario places with the same name in widely scattered areas, another good reason to have a map at hand. It's possible to start off on the wrong track entirely unless you are alert to this. If your ancestor's death certificate, or obituary, says he was born in York, does it mean the Town of York (now Toronto), or the County of York, a considerably larger area? Does it mean York, one of the former nine townships in York County, or was it the village of York in Seneca Township, Haldimand County?

Here are only a few examples of hundreds of multiple place-name occurrences:

Perth	— county in south central Ontario
	— county town of Lanark County
Prescott	— county along the Ottawa River
	— town in Augusta Township, Grenville County
Clinton	— township in Lincoln County
	— village in Goderich Township, Huron County
Hamilton	— city in Wentworth County
	— township in Northumberland County
Simcoe	— county west of Lake Simcoe
	— county town of Norfolk County

Some original townships (a few examples are Dumfries, Zorra, Oxford, Tilbury, Sandwich) were later subdivided into East, West, North, or South. The Township of Camden is in Kent County; the Township of Camden East is in Lennox & Addington County. Huron Township is not in Huron County, Brant Township is not in Brant County, and Haldimand Township is not in Haldimand County. Oxford Township is in Grenville County, but Oxford East, West, and North Townships are in Oxford County!

When the province was first being surveyed, some early townships were hastily numbered to accommodate the large numbers of arriving Loyalists and soldiers who needed land. As a result, some early land records may have such reference as "the third township from the lake", or "the Quaker Township". In an area now included in parts of Hastings, Addington, Frontenac, and Prince Edward Counties, some townships were first numbered:

3

1	Kingston	6	Sophiasburg
2	Ernestown	7	Ameliasburg
3	Fredericksburg	8	Sydney
4	Adolphustown	9	Thurlow
5	Marysburg	10	Richmond
		11	Camden

Some village or town names have disappeared through change or annexation by a larger municipality. Here, a gazetteer or local history will be valuable. Three volumes of *Places in Ontario, Their Names, Origins, and History* published by Mika Publishing (see Appendix II) make useful and interesting reading. A few of the larger centres with name changes are:

Present name	Former name
Ottawa	Bytown
Cornwall	New Johnstown
Toronto	York
Kitchener	Berlin
Burlington	Wellington Square
Dundas	Coote's Paradise
Niagara-on-the-Lake	Newark
Windsor	Sandwich
Cambridge	Galt, Hespeler, Preston

LOCATING
PROPERTY
DESCRIPTION

Once you've located your family, you will eventually want to pin down their exact location or property description in a town or township, because land records are often the only source of genealogical information in the earliest days. Sources for the property description might be the Computerized Land Records Index (if a Crown land grant was involved), an Agricultural Schedule of a census return, or documents found using the town/township Deeds Index.

Historical atlases for Ontario counties can be another source for a property description. Many, not all, of these atlases show township maps with property owners' names. However, these names are usually of owners at or near the publication date of the atlas, not of the original grantees.

Where a town or city is the location, a directory with street addresses may be the best source. An address can then lead to the legal property description on Land Registry plans. Assessment rolls, if available, will serve the same purpose.

FINDING
EMIGRANTS'
ORIGINS

Another goal in the ancestor hunt is to learn the previous residence or overseas *origin* of the immigrant to Ontario so that research can continue in another province or country. Ontario records, like those of any other "new world" country, have limitations in this respect. Such records as census returns, death certificates, or marriage certificates, will likely state birthplace as merely "U.S." or "Scotland". You are going to need the name of a town, village, or parish to be able to research elsewhere successfully.

Sources that should be investigated for this clue are cemetery inscriptions, obituaries, land petitions, military lists, Loyalist Claims, ships' lists, wills, and local histories, directories, and historical atlases. Chances are you may never discover exactly what you want, but perseverance is the only course. Just as an example, searches of all these records had failed to indicate where in Ireland one original emigrant had lived, other than "County Tyrone" in his land petition. Ironically, and by chance, we learned that the local school in his area had been named for the parish in Ireland.

Organizing and Filing Your Records
In organizing the material you collect, try to keep impeccable notes. From the outset it's important to record not only all the details of a document, but also to record its exact source. Systematic organization is thoroughly described in such books as Wright and Pratt's *Genealogical Research Essentials*, or Jonasson's *Untangling the Tree: Organizational Systems for the Family Historian*. Most genealogical textbooks have such a section.

A good test of your system is to see if someone else can look at your files and understand what you've done and where you're going next.

You should get used to evaluating the evidence that you find. In other words, consider your source. What your great-uncle Ned told you, and what the officiating minister at the wedding wrote, are not the same kind of sources. Keep an open, enquiring mind.

PRIMARY SOURCES

Records made *at the time of the event*, by someone involved in the event, or a witness to it, are considered primary sources or evidence. Usually this includes birth certificates, baptismal records, marriage records, death certificates, relationships in wills, cemetery inscriptions, and some census information, etc. In the next chapters we will look at these sources more critically.

SECONDARY SOURCES

Secondary sources (sometimes referred to as "circumstantial" evidence) mean records that were made some time *after* an event occurred, not necessarily by an involved party or witness. This can

5

include "hearsay" or family traditions, undocumented family histories and other such published material, and any information on a record or document given by an uninvolved party.

The genealogist tries to collect as much primary information as possible, but too often we find missing records and gaps in those records we have discovered. Then we rely on as much secondary material as is available.

If you're aware of the limitations of records groups and documents you're more likely to keep that open mind while searching. We want to stress that almost every source should be regarded with a healthy objectivity until it's reinforced with data from other sources. If we may quote Patricia Kennedy in *Families*, Vol. 16, No. 4, (1977), p. 198, "Do not blindly trust an isolated record."

PEDIGREE

As with any genealogical research, in Ontario you will want to trace back from the known to the unknown. The records you use and the steps you take will depend on your starting information. Working your way back in time from one generation to the previous one, painstaking and frustrating as it may be at times, is the only logical and acceptable way to plot your pedigree. By *pedigree* we mean your direct ancestors only, male and female, in each generation. This is a fundamental, or skeletal, chart.

Ideally, basic data on the pedigree for each ancestor will be his/her name with date and place of birth, marriage, and death. In the absence of primary sources, as aforementioned, circumstantial evidence should be gathered from all available secondary sources. In order to progress back each generation, proof of relationship, *identification*, is needed. Normally this would mean proving the parents of each ancestor, through birth/baptismal records, marriage records, wills, etc.

You may only be interested in developing a straight-line or single line pedigree, a different goal. This follows just one parent in each generation. Searching out one family at a time is obviously less confusing and makes orderly notekeeping easier.

GENEALOGY

Then there is the genealogical chart which traces all the descendants of one pair of ancestors. Brothers and sisters in each generation are included, with their spouses and children. The written form of such a chart is a true genealogy that systematically records all known data on each person. A widely accepted form for constructing and numbering a genealogy is that used in the National Genealogy Society's (U.S.) *Quarterly* or as described in Gilbert Doane's *Searching For Your Ancestors.*

GROUP SHEET

A common method of "storing" acquired information is the *family group sheet* whereby each male ancestor is shown on one page with his wife and children and all their relevant data. This is a convenient way to summarize or communicate family information.

FAMILY HISTORY

A family history goes beyond the basic data of the above goals, comprising a story of each generation built upon basic data, supplemented with all available additional information (geographical, historical, social, occupational, etc.) that will make long-gone ancestors "come alive" in appropriate context.

A family history has more appeal to a larger readership, not only to relatives but to others interested in the locality. If one of your goals is to publish, remember that most non-genealogists are turned off by a litany of names and dates, even though your scholarship may be admirable.

Whatever your goal as an end result of your research, please consider *donating a copy* of your publication, typed manuscript, or even your notes to a genealogical society, archives, or library in the area where your family lived. These groups and institutions have made it possible for you to collect your information, and they have not always been treated well by eager genealogists. Help us build good relationships with our archivists and librarians by returning to them some of the fruits of your labours.

REFERENCE TERMS, ABBREVIATIONS

The use of the term *Finding Aid* refers to readily available, on-site, archival reference aids that list or describe contents of a collection of records. *Inventories* and *Calendars* are specific types of finding aids relevant to the structure of particular records collections. The abbreviations *MG* (Manuscript Group) and *RG* (Record Group) are also widely used in archival cataloguing.

RESOURCE CENTRES

Abbreviations used for *resource centres* in the next chapters, notably after the subject headings, are listed in Appendix I. All repositories which hold copies of records are not mentioned, but the main research centres are listed here. Special local collections of manuscript and published material have not been included since they are numerous and widespread. We suggest that as you proceed in your research you should become familiar with local collections of interest to your specific locality.

Exact references to many records groups have not been included, as a personal visit to the Public Archives of Canada (PAC) or Archives of Ontario (AO) necessarily involves some orientation time. For example, after registration at AO, the Archivist will give some instruction on learning the double cataloguing system. Most records sought at AO by genealogists are easily accessible in the Reading Room itself. At PAC you will be directed to the *Division* you need (Manuscripts, Federal Archives, Maps, Library, etc.). In both centres lockers are provided because you cannot bring briefcases and other personal belongings into the Reading Rooms.

Most of the records groups are not "perfect" in their geographical coverage, their survival rate, nor in the amount of family information given. Generally speaking, the earlier the time period, the fewer records we have to work with. The challenge and satisfaction in genealogical research lie in finding and using all the accessible records to re-form your ancestor's family.

Immigrants working at a railway-building bush camp at the turn of the century.

8

1/ The Ontario Genealogical Society

The Ontario Genealogical Society (OGS) was founded in 1961 to serve the interests of genealogy and family history in this province. It has grown to become one of the largest such groups in North America. There are branches of OGS representing nearly every part of Ontario, each with its own newsletter, other publications, meetings, and projects.

At the main office in Toronto the Executive, Council, and Committee meetings are held; correspondence, memberships, and distribution of publications are handled. In effect, this is our central core. The Office Administrator and staff do not do research, but will answer a query with general information. The emphasis in OGS has always been a "do-it-yourself" approach to genealogy.

MEMBERSHIP

Membership benefits include the quarterly journal *Families*, the quarterly newsletter *Newsleaf*, and a choice of purchasable publications. The latter range from *Directory of Surnames* (members' research interests) and *Membership List* to research sources and aids. Members are allowed some free queries each year in "The Name Game", a *Families* feature for contacting others of mutual ancestral interest.

FAMILIES

In the following pages there will be many references to articles in *Families*, written by experts on sources that we all need to use for information. This quarterly, because of its continuity and the calibre of contributors, must be considered of prime value to anyone pursuing genealogy in Ontario. Back issues are available through the central office in Toronto.

LIBRARY

The Society's Library is housed in the Canadiana Section of the North York Public Library at Fairview Mall in Willowdale, part of Metropolitan Toronto (see address in Appendix I). Holdings are *non-circulating*. The staff at the library cannot undertake to do research.

BRANCHES

Branch membership gives access to more localized source information and contacts. Each branch has a newsletter, and many branches have published guides to their own areas (see Appendix II).

SEMINAR

The highlight of the year is the annual *Seminar*, three days of lectures, workshops, and socializing. The seminar is also open to non-members. Each year a different branch is the host, offering its guests some focus on that area's resources but also a variety of topics to appeal to all attendees. None of us should underestimate this opportunity for personal contact with fellow members and expert speakers. Seminar registrants will receive the *Seminar Annual*, a compendium of the weekend contributions and related material. This publication is also available through the OGS central office for purchase.

PROJECTS

Special on-going, long-range projects involving every branch of the Society are the transcriptions of some 4,500 cemeteries in Ontario, now 50% completed, and indexing of the 1871 census which should be completed by 1986. Cemetery transcriptions can be seen at the Public Archives of Canada (PAC) in Ottawa, at the Archives of Ontario (AO) in Toronto, and at the OGS Library. Many recorded cemeteries have been microfilmed, so they are accessible through Interlibrary Loan. The *Inventory of Recorded Cemeteries in Ontario* can be bought through the OGS central office. Many branches are selling, for a nominal sum, completed local transcriptions.

An Index to the 1871 Census transcription will also be available through the OGS central office.

(Photo courtesy of Marie Charbonneau)

10

2/ Vital Statistics Post-1869 (RGO)

CERTIFICATES

From 1 July 1869 births, marriages, and deaths were *supposed* to be registered with the provincial government. This didn't always happen, especially in the first years, for various reasons. An application for a "genealogical" certificate (which gives more information than the "short" form) presently costs $5.00 and you must supply name(s), date, and place for each event, along with your relationship to the party/parties. The more details you can supply, the greater your chance of obtaining a certificate. The fee includes a five-year search, two years on either side of the given year.

Indexes to vital statistics are not open to public access so your application depends on, as well as the details you've supplied, the discernment of the clerk at the Registrar General's Office, not only in searching the index, but also on the transcription of the record. Two applications for a death certificate for the same person, made at different times, have been known to produce certificates with conflicting information.

A *negative search notice* in lieu of the expected certificate could mean that you didn't forward enough details to identify the party/parties, or occasionally it could be clerical error. Try again when you've got more information.

Under its mandate, the Registrar General's Office does not exist to serve genealogists; it is clear that information given is a privilege, not a right.

DEATHS

Under Ontario law, death certificates do not reveal cause of death; under certain medical circumstances such information may be released. Before 1907, parents are normally not named on a death certificate. On other certificates you will often find missing information such as "birthplace" or "parents" because the party/parties to the event left it out or answered "unknown".

MUNICIPAL
OFFICES

Municipal clerks were required to keep records of vital statistics in their locality, whence came the returns to the provincial government. Not all of their copybooks have survived, but some municipal offices have them back to the 1890's. However, this is *restricted information* and according to the Vital Statistics Act, a clerk cannot show these records to anyone nor confirm any information in them. It is a mistake to think that this is an alternate source for vital statistics. Your request must go to the Registrar General.

DIVORCE RECORDS

Strictly speaking, divorce is a court function but is included here as a relatively recent vital statistic. Since 1931 divorces have been registered at the RGO *which does not issue copies*. Filing for divorce is done in the county of residence, so the County Court Clerk could issue a copy of the judgment.

JUDGMENTS

AO now holds Divorce Court records 1931-1959 but indexes to the records remain at the local courthouse. AO can also supply a copy of the judgment but first you must obtain the year and file number from the County Court Clerk, likely involving a personal visit to search the index. This index is chronological by date of filing the suit, and alphabetical by name within each year. Needless to say, there is much sensitive information in a divorce file, most of which will not be accessible.

Prior to 1931 divorce could only be granted by an Act of the Canadian Parliament, and information should be sought from the Clerk of the Senate (see Appendix I).

Prior to Confederation in 1867 divorce was also granted by a legislative Act, and these can be found only by checking the subject matter of Acts passed each year. Because of the time and expense incurred by the system before 1931, not everyone in such a situation followed the official procedure. A separation agreement may have been reached, but in many cases where one partner simply vanished, it's unlikely that this step was taken.

ADOPTION

In Ontario, adoption records are private and closed. Seeking this kind of information, you could try the Ontario government's Voluntary Adoption Disclosure Registry (see Appendix I). There are also self-help groups such as Parent Finders that work throughout North America.

Office of the
Registrar
General

Ontario

Macdonald Block
Parliament Buildings
Toronto, Ontario
M7A 1Y5

416/965-1687

416/965-6749

83-549993-5-01
--- BRENDA MERRIMAN
--- R.R. #1
--- PUSLINCH, ONTARIO

NOB 2J0

INFORMATION EXTRACTED FOR GENEALOGY

MARRIAGE

PLACE OF MARRIAGE: GLENGARRY

DATE OF MARRIAGE: JULY 15,1884

	GROOM	BRIDE
NAME:	MCMILLAN, HUGH	MCINTOSH, ANNIE
AGE:	27	25
PLACE OF BIRTH:	LOCHIEL	CHARLOTTENBURGH
RELIGION:	PRESBY.	PRESBY.

PARENTS NAMES
    FATHER: MCMILLAN, ARCHIBALD   MCINTOSH, JOHN
    MOTHER: GRANT, MARGARET   MCDONALD, CATHERINE

WITNESSES: DUNCAN T. MCINTOSH
    MARGARET ANN MCKAY

OFFICIATING CLERGY: ALEX MACPHERSON

REGISTRATION NUMBER: 1884-05-011169

ISSUED AT TORONTO
DECEMBER 2,1983

(MRS) K.V. BELL

MANAGER, CUSTOMER SERVICES

A "genealogical" marriage certificate from the Office of the Registrar-General.

3/ Vital Statistics Pre-1869
(PAC, AO, Church Archives, Churches)

CHURCH
REGISTERS

When you are looking for proof of births, marriages, and deaths before civil registration began, you will only find this in church registers, as baptisms, marriages, and burials. In some cases the birthdate is given as well as baptismal date. On the whole, burial registers were poorly kept and often non-existent.

Finding appropriate church records for a family may be easier said than done. The procedure "from scratch" may be described as: a) learning their location, b) learning their religious affiliation (census is a good source), c) names of local churches/missions/circuits/ministers of the time period through historical reference, d) learning if the registers still exist and where they are currently located.

Some early church records remain with the original church when it's still in use. Some have been lost. In the case of a church being closed, they may have been sent to another church in the area or to a central church archives. Some records were part of a larger mission or circuit, so other neighbouring place-names must be noted.

To make a very generalized point, there is more chance of finding records from the larger denominations. Small denominations and congregations that died out or amalgamated with another sect may take all your powers of sleuthing to trace.

UNITED CHURCH

To those unfamiliar with the history of Canadian churches, we must mention that the *United Church of Canada* was a union formed in 1925 of Methodist, Congregational, the majority of Presbyterian churches, and a few small denominations. The Archives of the United Church (see Appendix I) has collected some early records for all these denominations, but some Presbyterian records will be found at PCA (see Appendix I) as well.

TRANSCRIBED/
PUBLISHED
REGISTERS

Registers of many early historic churches have been transcribed and/or published, deposited at resource centres. PAC has published a *Checklist of Parish Registers* (1981) which lists church registers available there, many of which are on microfilm. Baxter's *In Search of Your Roots* lists many parish registers available at central church archives, particularly Anglican (Church of England) and United Church of Canada (Methodist, Congregational, Presbyterian, etc). Some published church registers are listed in *Some Ontario References and Sources for the Family Historian*. This book also lists Anglican Diocesan Offices and Roman Catholic Archdiocesan Offices in Ontario.

The LDS (Mormon) Church has completed the microfilming of most pre-1910 Roman Catholic church registers in Ontario, with the exception of those in the Diocese of Alexandria and a few other churches.

There is no easy way to deal with locating the register you need. Check catalogues of various repositories and/or correspond with the minister of an individual church. Most large denominations publish an annual report or directory with names and addresses of churches. *Please* do not expect a minister/priest/church officer to give you free search time for your ancestors. Enclose a token money order as a goodwill gesture with your stamped, self-addressed envelope. Please note that *only* Canadian stamps can be used in Canada; otherwise use an International Postal Reply Coupon. Most church archives, like many public institutions, don't have the staff to handle requests by mail, although they may indicate whether the records you want are there.

For descriptions of church archives of various denominations (Roman Catholic, Anglican, United, Presbyterian, and Baptist) see *Readings in Ontario Genealogical Sources*.

A highly recommended article is "Utility and Variety of Early Church Records" by Bruce Elliott in *Families*, Vol. 16, No. 4 (1977).

CEMETERIES

Cemetery inscriptions can provide evidence that may not be found elsewhere — date of death, age at death, and sometimes, fortuitously, place of birth. To begin with, you must know where your ancestor lived (and died), and learn where the local cemeteries are.

However it may not be necessary to visit the actual site. First you should check whatever transcriptions have been made, through one of the three main repositories where all completed OGS transcriptions are deposited. Also, a local OGS Branch may be selling its transcriptions for a nominal charge.

The drawbacks are that the headstone that you seek may have succumbed to years of weathering; and we're dealing with secondary evidence to a certain extent. Certainly the date of death would be primary evidence, normally supplied by a relative who had been nearby when death occurred. But that same relative, whether widow(er) or child, may not have had true knowledge of age and place of birth, especially if the latter was in a country unfamiliar to the informant.

OBITUARIES

Looking for an *obituary* is a natural adjunct to finding a death date. If a local newspaper exists for that date, you may find a published tribute. This seems to occur more frequently when the deceased was a pioneer or a prominent citizen. The best obituaries often mention previous origins, arrival here, occupation, community involvement, surviving family and their locations. Other times you may find only a simple death notice, possibly with place of interment.

NEWSPAPER INDEXING

AO has a fine collection of 19th and 20th century newspapers for southern Ontario. The Newspaper Division of the National Library is preparing a list of newspapers that have been indexed for vital statistics notices. Many local libraries and OGS Branches are also involved in such indexing projects.

RELIGIOUS NEWSPAPER NOTICES

Many religions started denominational newspapers and periodicals which regularly featured birth, marriage, and death notices or obituaries. Some notable examples are the Wesleyan Methodist *Christian Guardian* (at UCA, nominal index from 1829 for early years); the *Catholic Register* (RCA, AO, not indexed); the *Christian Messenger*, later called *Canadian Baptist* (indexed by Hamilton Branch OGS from 1854); and the *Presbyterian Record* (at PCA from 1844, unindexed).

Publication of notices from some denominational and other newspapers can be found in the already mentioned Hunterdon House books by Reid, Wilson, and McKenzie.

METHODIST BAPTISMAL REGISTERS

From the 1840's Wesleyan Methodist ministers were required by their church to submit baptismal returns, which were copied into a central register. This is a case where the register is a third copy of the event. Arranged by township/town/city up until the 1890's, these entries can prove to be a real treasure. Generally they show name of the child, date of birth and baptism, parents' names and residence, and name of minister.

The pages of these registers, as you read them in order of entry, are not necessarily in chronological order. Now microfilmed, they must be viewed personally at the UCA.

DISTRICT MARRIAGE REGISTERS

District Marriage Registers were created by district Clerks of the Peace from 1793 but early entries were few, made only if the couple paid to enter a copy of their marriage certificate. After 1831 this form of civil registration was compulsory for "dissenting" denominations which had been given the right to perform marriages that year.

Surviving registers begin at different dates and generally continue until 1858 when county registers were established. To use a district register — and most are indexed — you must know your location and then determine which district covered this. The following district registers are available at AO on microfilm (there is a Finding Aid filed under *Department of the Provincial Secretary*, Appendix F):

Bathurst	Gore
Brock	Home
Colborne	Ottawa
Huron	Prince Edward
Johnstown	Talbot
London	Victoria
Newcastle	

Western and Eastern District registers have been published in *The Ontario Register*, Vols. 1-4. The remaining district registers are being serialized beginning in Vol. 6. Entirely missing are those for Midland and Niagara. Information contained in the registers is minimal — names of parties, place and date of marriage, denomination, witnesses.

COUNTY MARRIAGE REGISTERS

County Marriage Registers began in 1858, no longer based on the obsolete district, and continued until civil registration began in 1869. Some continue to a later date, and some have the occasional baptismal register. These registers include marriages of *all* denominations.

INDEXES

A series of indexes to these is being published by Generation Press (see Appendix II) with the warning that the registers themselves are *second copies* of the original records, so that indexing was actually done as a third transcription. Obviously this leaves room for error, beginning with the minister when he made the original entry, and when he made copies for the government at the end of each year. There are currently 14 published indexes, with 28 still to be done.

There is more information here than in district registers — names and ages of parties, residence, birthplace, parents' names (often the mother's birthname), date and place of marriage, denomination, and witnesses. AO holds the original and

Return   *Kenneth Maclennan*

BRIDEGROOM.					NAME.
NAME.	Age.	RESIDENCE.	PLACE OF BIRTH.	NAMES OF PARENTS.	
James Keith	24	Pickering	Aberdeen	Alexander Keith Mary Mitchell	Jean Pat...
Alexander McIntosh	30	Pickering	Nairnshire	Wm McIntosh Eliza Ross	Anne G...
Thomas Stephenson	21	Pickering	Pickering	Thomas Stephenson Mary Matthews	Rachel...
George Henis	28	Whitby	England	Henry Henis Sarah Bolin	Mary Ann...

*I hereby certify that the foregoing is a true and correct Statement of a...
preceding the date hereof
Whitby Jany 1st 1862.*

A County marriage register entry.

microfilmed registers, and the same Finding Aid applies as above.

JUSTICE OF THE PEACE

A few further notes are in order before we leave vital statistics. A marriage neither found in local church records, nor in the above registers, may have been performed by a *Justice of the Peace*. Some are found in pre-1831 district registers if the couple paid the registration fee; after 1831 there are fewer found in district registers. The odd collection of such records may be found in main repositories catalogued under "Marriage Records" or geographical place-name material.

In the earliest days of the province only the Church of England and the Roman Catholic Church were authorized to perform marriages. In a district with fewer than five Anglican clergymen, a Justice of the Peace was allowed to marry couples who lived more than 18 miles from the nearest clergyman. Gradu-

(OA, RG 8, Vol. 4, Series 1-6-B)

ally other denominations were "recognized", many not until 1831 or later. Many of these may have performed their own marriage rites before this, and the Marriage Act of 1858 "legalized" them. When you reach a dead end for a marriage source, it's always wise to look at Anglican registers for the area.

BONDS, LICENCES

Marriage Bonds record the names of parties who obtained a marriage licence rather than being married after publication of banns in a church. This collection 1803-1845 is indexed, available at both PAC and AO. The bond will tell names of the parties *intending* to marry, residence, and date of bond. You can't always assume that a marriage followed. Also, *not* every marriage by licence will be included in this series.

The Ontario Archives also has some collections of individuals' marriage licences 1853-1911; the Finding Aid has a surname index.

4/ Census Returns
(PAC, AO, OGS, Univ Lib, LDS)

Finding ancestors in census returns helps to fill out your family groups and sometimes adds a generation. Here you will learn their religious affiliation for help in searching out church records. Before 1842, a census was taken annually by township assessors and filed with the District Clerk of the Peace. Few of these have survived, and they have little information, other than helping you to establish a residence for a head of household. Most that survive are at AO in the Municipal Records series (see Chapter 8). OGS plans to publish the Finding Aid for this series in 1985.

Returns for *1842* named heads of families only, but they did include age statistics on family members, and agricultural information. This census has not survived for all townships (see Appendix III).

From *1851* to *1881* the decennial census named all members of the household with age, place of birth, occupation, religious affiliation, marital status, and in the 1871 and 1881 returns, a column for "origin" which indicated the ethnic heritage of the father of each person. As an example of how this column can help identify people, in one family the husband's "origin" was English, the wife was Irish, the two older children French, and remaining children English. This helped confirm family tradition that the wife had previously been married to a French-Canadian, and had children by him.

Note here that the 1851 Census was actually taken in January of 1852.

The *1891* census is not expected to be released to public access until 1991 because of the federal government's "right to privacy" policy. The *Index to Census of Canada (Ontario)* at PAC and AO will point out the microfilm number you want.

Not all returns for all areas have survived; an unfortunate example is the 1851 census for Toronto and York County. The census is arranged by towns/townships, so this information is your essential starting point.

AGE

Some concerns to remember are that we don't know who gave the information to the enumerator. The informant may have guessed at some ages. Age is commonly faulty information, either deliberate or inadvertent. Early returns asked for "age at next birthday" but by 1871 "present age" was recorded.

The informant may not have known place of birth of some family members, and made a guess.

BIRTHPLACE

Some abbreviations used for birth in Ontario are:

O. (Ontario)	U.C. (Upper Canada)
C.W. (Canada West)	E.C. (English Canada)

Birthplace referred to simply as "*F*" in 1851 does *not* mean "foreign-born"; it generally refers to "French", and in this context generally infers French-Canadian. Strangely enough, "F" can also indicate "of British parentage", as emphatically stated by a census official in the 1851 census of Camden East.

NAMES

Nicknames can obscure an ancestor's name as you know it, e.g. "Nancy" for Ann, "Minnie" for Melinda or Wilhelmina, and countless other variations. "George" or "George H." listed as a child, may have been known as "Henry" all his adult life. The enumerator has been known to exercise wild license in the spelling of a surname.

When you've found your family, don't stop at that point. You never know when you might find another family a little farther on. You might as well finish the whole town/township for other surname occurrences. Of course the record won't specify relationships between families; you'll have to seek other proof.

RELIGION

Religious affiliation can be considered accurate information; watch for a wife's differing from her husband's. To find their marriage record you may have to look at both sources. You may notice a change in affiliation from one census year to another which could affect children's baptisms. Most frustrating is the family that lists "No Creed" for the religion column. The only hope is to locate an older generation, perhaps in an earlier census, which is still affiliated with organized religion. Some abbreviations used in this column are:

WM (Wesleyan Methodist)	FRIENDS (Quaker)
EM (Episcopal Methodist)	EL (Evangelical
CS, KS (Church/Kirk of	Lutheran)
Scotland)	BC (Bible Christian)
UP (United Presbyterian)	C, CONG (Congregational)
D, T (Dunkard or Tunker)	MENN (Mennonite)
NC (Methodist New	EUB (Evangelical
Connexion)	United Brethren)
CP, C Presb (Canada	
Presbyterian)	

CANADIAN FAMILY
CENSUS FORM
1842 - 1881

1842 p.	Name														Real Property			5-7		Occup		8		Total no.	9

1842
p.

Name 4

Real Property 5-7

Occup 8

Total no. 9

Birth-places 11-17

Yrs. in prov. 18

Religion 46-61

20 5 & <		5-14		Males 14-18		18-21		21-30		30-60		60 & >		Females 14-45		45 & > 37		Acres occupied	69	Acres improved	70	
m	f	m	f	m	s	m	s	m	s	m	s	m	s	m	s	m	s	Tenure	89	Children 5-16	120

Twp. Co

Names				Occups	Birthplaces	Religion	Res	Age	M S	Other	House Type/Comments

1852
Div.
p.

Twp. Co

1861
Div.
p.

Twp. Co

Names				Age	Birthplaces	Religion	Origin	Occupations		M S	Other/Comments

1871
Div.
p.
Line

Twp. Co

1881
Div.
p.

Twp. Co

© 1984 Ontario Genealogical Society

Sample of OGS Census Form

22

DEATHS

Don't neglect the column of *Deaths* in 1851 (deaths during 1851, age and cause), 1861 (deaths during 1860, age and cause), and Schedule of Deaths in 1871 which follows returns of the "Living" (month of death within last 12 months, age, birthplace, religion, marital status, and cause of death).

AGRICULTURAL
SCHEDULE

Also look for the *Agricultural* Schedule which will give you the property description of the family residence, and an idea of their standard of living (number of animals, farm produce, etc).

In 1853 a special census was taken by the provincial Department of Agriculture, of some immigrants who had arrived within the past 45-50 years. It is not known now how many of these were actually returned, and only 41 have survived. The information on the returns tells, among other things, the parish, post town, county, and country from which he emigrated, his occupation there, date of arrival in Canada, age, marital status, and present location.

These are stored at PAC (Records Group Division) from which you can obtain a copy of the names and their locations, or an individual's return, by quoting reference *RG 17 Vol. 2325*. OGS *Newsleaf*, Vol. 11, No. 2 (June 1981) published the list of 41 names.

Some local census returns have been transcribed and/or indexed by Historical Societies and OGS Branches. OGS has a comprehensive census form for sale that allows you to record one family from 1842 to 1881.

A pioneer homestead near Renfrew, Ontario.

23

5/ Land Records

A) Computerized Land Records Index — CLRI (AO, PAC, OGS, LDS)

Prepared by the Archives of Ontario, this most useful tool for genealogists is now widely available in genealogical and other major libraries, usually in convenient microfiche form. It is the only province-wide index dating from first official settlement. The CLRI summarizes original land grants from the Crown, derived from the initial grants, Canada Company sales and leases, and grants to the Peter Robinson settlers. It does *not* include subsequent transactions on any piece of property.

This index can be searched either by surname or by township name. *Always search every spelling variation of your surname.* What it will tell you, whenever the information was available from the original record, is a property description, date and type of grant, and type of transaction. The Date Identity Code and Type of Grant are sometimes overlooked, but can provide you with some good clues for research.

TYPE OF
FREE GRANT

Type of Free Grant includes these abbreviations:

OR	(Old Regulations)	ME	(Military
NR	(New Regulations)		Emigrant)
FF	(Full Fees)	LB	(Land Board)
UE	(Loyalist)	PR	(Peter Robinson
DUE	(Daughter of		Settler)
	Loyalist)	SE	(Scotch Emigrant)
SUE	(Son of Loyalist)	AA	(Hardship Grant)
MC	(Military	1819	Regulations
	Claimant)	1820	"
COMM	(Heir & Devisee	1825	"
	Commission)	V	(Veteran-Fenian,
M	(Militia)		South African
			War)

These designations can lead to other collections of records or material at AO or elsewhere; they refer to regulations by which a grant was given. Loyalists, disbanded soldiers of the Crown, and certain government officials, as well as most immigrants up to 1827 had the right to free land grants, the amount of which varied according to their qualifications and the current regulations. Other settlers, especially later, had to buy their lands. Regulations changed often over the years.

Many of these designations will be mentioned in this and following Chapters. A Hardship Grant was one where fees and/or costs were waived when it was proved that the settler was barely subsisting, hence the name "Hardship".

There were several steps in the granting process, all of which involved documents in different government departments. Some of these were petitions, location tickets, assignments, Orders-in-Council, fiats, and warrants; some discussion of these as pertaining to genealogy will follow later. All *original* documents are now at AO except Upper Canada Land Petitions and records of the first Heir and Devisee Commission, which are at PAC.

The *Date Identity Code* in the CLRI includes these numbered categories:

DATE IDENTITY CODE

1 (location)	5 (sale)
2 (assignment)	6 (contract)
3 (patent)	7 (deed)
4 (lease)	8 (Order-in-Council)

It should be noted that it is normally much more difficult to find information on a person who appears as "leasing" land. You may be able to go on and find a petition for him, or you may find something in Township Papers, but if he never became a *landowner* you will likely find little evidence of him in land records. This is particularly true when you're investigating deeds, as many leases and rental of properties were informal and unregistered agreements.

In *Families*, Vol. 14, No. 4 (1975), John Mezaks, Supervisor of Government Records at AO, has an article called "Crown Grants in the Home District: The System and the Existing Records". Although prepared for a Seminar on the Home District, the article covers the system of land regulations for all of Upper Canada. This is an excellent reference for understanding the intricacies of types of grants. See also Patricia Kennedy's article "Records of the Land Settlement Process: Pre-Confederation", in *Families*, Vol. 16, No. 4 (1977).

B) Upper Canada Land Petitions (PAC, AO)

A petition to the government for a land grant was the beginning of the process to acquire ownership of a piece of Crown land. PAC holds the originals; both PAC and AO have microfilm copies. A person might petition shortly after arrival here while temporarily living in a town or with relatives, or he might find a suitable piece of land and begin to settle immediately, applying later for the grant.

Some petitions are very straightforward and give little information about the petitioner, other than his presence in the province at that date. Others may give their arrival date in Canada, their birthplace, marital status, number in family, or any eligibility for a special type of grant. When sons and daughters of Loyalists petitioned for their free land grant, they gave their father's name to support their claim. Many times oaths of allegiance to the Crown are included with petitions or affidavits from character witnesses.

The petitions are indexed by surname and this is another case where you should search all variant spellings. In those days people were not as particular as we are about spelling the family name. Illiteracy was common, so the local scribe who penned the petition was free to use his own interpretation and phonetic spelling.

PROPERTY
DESCRIPTION

You'll seldom find property descriptions in a petition unless the petitioner was already on the property and asking for a patent to it. However, if a petition was "recommended" by the Executive Council, its date can often be connected with an entry and location on the CLRI.

LAND BOOKS

On the Index to petitions are also references to Land Books which record their receipt in Executive Council Minutes. Useful reading: "Deciphering the Upper Canada Land Books and Land Petitions" by Patricia Kennedy in *Readings in Ontario Genealogical Sources*.

Men petitioning for *military* or *militia* claims will state the name of their regiment or company with dates of service. Where service in the regular British Army is involved, this is a perfect lead to British War Office records at the Public Record Office in London (and on microfilm through the LDS Library).

AO has an exclusive series of petitions, arranged alphabetically by surname, of requests made to the *Commissioner of Crown Lands* rather than to the Lieutenant Governor in Council as above, most of them post-1827.

C) Patents
(AO)

A patent was issued to an individual who successfully obtained a grant of Crown land, after a series of administrative procedures and the fulfillment of

PROVINCE OF CANADA.

VICTORIA, *by the Grace of God, of the United Kingdom of Great Britain and Ireland, QUEEN, Defender of the Faith.*

To all to whom these Presents shall come—**Greeting:**

Whereas *Kenneth Mac Kenzie of the Township of Puslinch in the County of Wellington, yeoman* hath contracted and agreed to and with Our Commissioner for the sale of Our Crown Lands, duly authorized by Us in this behalf, for the absolute purchase, at and for the price and sum of *Eighty one Pounds five Shillings* of lawful money of Our said Province, of the Lands and Tenements hereinafter mentioned and described, of which We are seized in right of Our Crown. NOW KNOW YE, that in consideration of the said sum of *Eighty one Pounds five Shillings* by *him* the said *Kenneth Mac Kenzie* to Our said Commissioner of Crown Lands, in hand well and truly paid to Our use, at or before the sealing of these Our Letters Patent, We have granted, sold, aliened, conveyed and assured, and by these Presents do grant, sell, alien, convey and assure, unto the said *Kenneth Mac Kenzie his* Heirs and Assigns **for ever,** All that Parcel or Tract of Land, situate, lying and being in the Town*ship* of *Puslinch* in the County of *Wellington* of Our said Province, containing by admeasurement *one hundred acres* be the same more or less ; which said Parcel or Tract of Land may be otherwise known as follows, that is to say : being composed of

The Rear or North East half of the late Clergy Reserve Lot number Seventeen in the Tenth Concession of the aforesaid Township of Puslinch

Recorded 21st Jany 1856

Dept Reg

To have and to hold the said Parcel or Tract of Land hereby granted, conveyed and assured, unto the said *Kenneth Mac Kenzie his* heirs and assigns for ever; saving, excepting and reserving, nevertheless unto Us, Our Heirs and Successors, all Mines of Gold and Silver, and the free uses, passage and enjoyment of, in, over and upon all navigable waters that shall or may be hereafter found on or under, or be flowing through or upon any part of the said Parcel or Tract of Land hereby granted as aforesaid.

G I V E N under the Great Seal of Our Province of Canada : **Witness,** Our Trusty and Well-beloved SIR EDMUND WALKER HEAD, Baronet, Governor General of British North America, and Captain General and Governor in Chief in and over Our Provinces of Canada, Nova Scotia, New Brunswick, and the Island of Prince Edward, and Vice-Admiral of the same, &c., &c., &c. At TORONTO, this *Seventh* day of *January* in the year of Our Lord, one thousand eight hundred and fifty-six, and in the *nineteenth* year of Our Reign.

By Command of His Excellency in Council.

Geo. Et. Cartier

Secretary.   *Commissioner of Crown Lands.*

Reg. No. *15796*
Doc. No. *2050*

A land patent dated 1856.
(Courtesy Public Archives Canada)

certain settlement duties. Although *certificates* for land were issued from 1783, it wasn't until 1795 that actual patents were issued. In that 12-year period various other documents were used as temporary substitutes, as mentioned in the CLRI section. Sometimes patents weren't issued until years after a grant.

INDEXES, COPIES

Patents have been indexed by *surname* 1795-1825 and by *township* up to 1850, on microfilm at AO, with indexes to the present day located at the Ontario Ministry of Natural Resources, Official Documents Section. The patents themselves are stored at the Official Documents Section, Ministry of Government Services, from which you can obtain a copy by giving them the property description and date of patent.

D) Heir and Devisee Commission (PAC, AO)

Records of the First Commission 1797-1804 are at PAC. Records of the Second Commission 1805-1911 are at AO. The job of the Commission was to clarify land titles where patents had not been issued. There were several reasons that could cause a claim to be made. When the original nominee for a Crown land grant had died, or left the property, an heir, devisee, or assignee had to apply to the Commission with proof of his right to the patent.

DOCUMENTS

Some of the supporting documents might include land certificates, location tickets, copies of wills, mortgages, deeds, receipts, affidavits, or letters. A patent would be issued to the claimant if the Commission accepted the evidence and if the Surveyor General's Office (up to 1827) or Crown Lands Office (after 1827) approved the validity of the original nominee's title.

These records are indexed alphabetically by surname of claimant. More detail can be found in *Families*, Vol. 16, No. 4 (1977), "Records of the Heir and Devisee Commission", by John Mezaks.

E) Township Papers (AO)

This group of records is arranged by township, concession, and lot number, so knowing the property description is essential to using them. These are papers referring to a specific lot and might contain a variety of documents or letters about claims to the property, and transfers of a claim prior to patenting.

A Finding Aid is available under "Crown Lands Department" (Appendix H). The entire series is being microfilmed by AO, so until they have finished, the Papers for some townships will be out of circulation.

F) Abstract Indexes to Deeds
(County Registry Offices, AO)

Subsequent land transactions, after the original patent, were and are registered at County Land Registry Offices and can be found by using the Abstract Index. Microfilm copies of these are at AO up to about 1958. Again, you must know the property description to search this, as they are arranged by township, concession, and lot number. In the case of a village, town, or city, they will be found by subdivision plan or street location.

INSTRUMENTS

From this Abstract you'll learn when an ancestor's name first appeared, the type of *instrument* or document (deed, bargain and sale, mortgage, quit claim, etc.), date of instrument, date of registry, grantee and grantor, and instrument number. *"Grantor"* is the person(s) giving the grant, or mortgaging the property; *"grantee"* is the person(s) receiving the grant or to whom the property might be mortgaged. Use the instrument number and date to look at the document itself, also found by name of township, village, town, etc.

Following the ancestral name(s) in the Abstract usually gives a good indication of arrival on and departure from (or death on) that property.

WILLS

Wills may be shown in the Abstract Index as registered land documents. This is an important source for unprobated wills that were used to transfer property. The instrument number of a will in this case refers, like the other documents, to the Registry Office number and not to Surrogate Court records. After 1865, wills which do not state a property description, and powers-of-attorney, are recorded in the General Registers series of each Registry Office (see below).

G) Deeds
(County Land Registry Offices, AO)

All deeds (from which the Abstract Index was created) are similarly registered at a County Land Registry Office. Many of these are on microfilm at AO up to about 1876. If you find an instrument number later than 1876, i.e. not microfilmed, you can obtain a copy from the appropriate Land Registry Office by quoting the instrument number and township name, for a nominal copying fee.

To His Excellency Francis Gore Esquire
Lieutenant Governor of the Province of
Upper Canada &c &c &c

In Council

The Petition of Charles Crowder of Osnabrugh Yeoman —

Humbly Sheweth

That your Petitioner is the Son of William Crowder
of Osnabrugh a loyalist U. E. has arrived at the
full age of twenty one years has taken the oaths of
Allegiance as will appear by the annexed Certificate
and has never received any land or order for land
from the Crown — Wherefore your Petitioner
prays your Excellency in Council will be pleased
to grant him two hundred acres of the Waste land
of the Crown and permit _____ to be
his Attorney to locate the same and receive the
Patent when Completed and your Petitioner will
ever pray —

Charles Crowder

Cornwall 6th July 1816 —

Eastern District. Before me Samuel Anderson Esquire
Chairman of the General Quarter Sessions of the
Peace assembled personally appeared Charles Crowder
the above named Petitioner and made oath that he is the
Person herein describes himself to be has arrived to
the full age of twenty one years and has never received
any land or order for land from the Crown —

Sworn before me in open Sessions
this 6th day of July 1816

S. Anderson Chairman

Charles + Crowder
his mark

Eastern District. We Samuel Anderson Esquire Chairman
and Archibald McLean Clerk of the Peace certify
that Charles Crowder personally appeared at the
General Quarter Sessions of the Peace this day is
recognized by the Magistrates to be the Son of William
Crowder of Osnabrugh who retained his Loyalty during
the late War without Suspicion of aiding or assisting the
Enemy and that the said William Crowder did his duty
in defence of the Province during the late War —

Dated at the Court House at Cornwall S. Anderson Chairman
in the said District this 6th day July 1816   Arch McLean
                                                Clerk of the Peace

A land petition dated 1816.
(Courtesy Norman Crowder)

30

Most documents will at least establish a date and place for your ancestor. From the early 1800's a wife was often named in a sale to bar her dower right, which helps identify a family. Occasionally other family relationships are mentioned.

COPY BOOKS

From 1797 when the land registration system was set up, until 1847, the exchange of property was normally registered as a "memorial" in County memorial or copy books. The memorial did not necessarily contain the full text of the original document, and for early days there is some doubt now as to where the originals were kept. It may be that the party/parties concerned kept them. Some, not all, copy books are indexed. These are arranged by *county*, not township. From 1847 a change in the system produced copy books of memorials recorded by *townships* (indexed for the first few years by surnames).

GENERAL REGISTERS

But there was also a *General Register*, copy book series after 1866 for each county which could include such land-related documents as wills and powers-of-attorney, etc. Reference numbers from such a Register *may* be located by county name, but collections don't exist for all counties at AO.

In 1865 Registry Offices stopped "memorializing" and began copying full text of documents. In 1955 copy books were discontinued entirely and are being distributed by AO to local archives, museums, libraries, etc. Copy books are useful when original documents are missing or not microfilmed.

Some other functions of the Registry Offices over the years have been the recording of naturalizations (see this heading later), railway debentures, bankruptcies, court judgments, and miscellaneous local reports. Any such volumes that are found are being distributed on loan to local institutions along with copy books. Any papers of a private rather than government nature will be eventually catalogued at AO.

ADDRESSES

OGS has for sale a booklet called *Land Records in Ontario Land Registry Offices* by David and Jean McFall, which goes into more detail about the land registration system. Included in it is "The History of the Land Record Copy Books" by Shirley Spragge, an explanation of this series of records, with a list of repositories presently storing some of them, current to about 1983. The 1984 edition of this booklet contains addresses of the county and district Land Registry Offices.

6/ Court Records

From 1793 there were two courts involved in the probate and administration of estates: *Surrogate Court* and *Probate Court*.

A) Probate Court
(AO)

PROBATE

The Probate Court had jurisdiction over estates involving property in more than one district and those of more than £5 value. In 1858 the Probate Court was abolished and the Surrogate Court became the only court dealing with deceased's estates, with jurisdiction by county of the property involved.

Probate Court records are at AO with a surname index. The actual files, all now microfilmed, may not show date of death. You might find a dated will and a notice with date of probate, so you can infer that death occurred between those dates.

B) Surrogate Court
(AO, local courthouses)

SURROGATE
PRE-1858

The Surrogate Court was first responsible for estates involving property in one district only. The system for filing and keeping these records varied from place to place, which explains how much or how little material you might find. Estate files from these pre-1858 Surrogate Court records are usually located, when they have survived, by name of a county which was part of the original district. For instance, Niagara District files are with Lincoln County in the AO card catalogue; Gore District with Wentworth County.

Abstracts from early *Kingston* and vicinity wills 1790-1858 have been published, as have *London* District wills 1800-1839 (see Appendix II).

By 1985 AO expects to complete a surname index to the Surrogate Court records 1793-1858, which will ease immeasurably a search for these early records. In addition, a list of all Surrogate Court records will be added to the Court Records Inventory with a guide to using the index of each county.

POST-1858
INDEXES

Surname indexes for most counties begin in 1858 when the Surrogate Court took over sole responsibility for probate and administration. The County indexes vary in content; some may give only a name and number; most give no indication of the year. Some will list two or three reference numbers, such as grant number, non-contentious business (NCB) number, and/or Registry Book number. You need to make an exact note of all numbers since there was no uniform indexing method for all counties. For the time being, a Finding Aid at AO under Court Records can tell you which number of several is the right one to locate the estate file for a particular county. Indexes generally extend to the 1960's.

FILES

Most original estate files up to 1939 are in the custody of AO, catalogued as above by county and indexed by surname. Files are microfilmed only to 1900. For a file dated between 1900-1939, which is kept in a different storage site, retrieval can be made with name of deceased, file number, and county of death. For files after 1939 the local county courthouse must be contacted. There are some current exceptions of County Courts that maintain their own files post-1900, such as Kent and Brant Counties.

LETTERS OF ADMINISTRATION

Material found in the files might include a *will* or *letters of administration*. The latter, where the deceased was intestate, does not have as much family information as a will. However, you will learn date and place of death, occupation, and property description(s) if applicable. More modern-day files might contain a list of heirs and next-of-kin with addresses. The name of the applicant for administering the estate appears of course; often this is the widow or a child, with the relationship specified.

WILLS

Almost everyone is familiar with the general form of a will. If a spouse isn't mentioned, it's likely that he/she predeceased the testator. *Not all children are necessarily mentioned in a will*. Older children may have received "benefits" before the will was made; estrangements have caused others to be left out deliberately.

A bonus in a will is reference to married daughters, or to grandchildren and other relatives. There are cases where a daughter-in-law is called a daughter, or similar ambiguous terminology. You might find an executor or witness with the same surname as the deceased, who is not mentioned in the text of the will, but possibly indicating a relationship.

INVENTORIES

Inventories, which list personal property, may be found with wills or administrations; inventories of real property were not microfilmed.

An interesting article for background study is "Wills and Inventories: Records of Life and Death in a Developing Society" by Brian S. Osborne in *Families*, Vol. 19, No. 4 (1980). A booklet on wills, by

Catherine Shepard, published by OGS, contains detailed basic information.

We have already described how many *unprobated wills* are found with land records (see Chapter 5, Section F, Abstract Indexes to Deeds). If you don't find a will in court records, this is an essential search.

Not finding a will or administration for an ancestor in the county where he's known to have died, likely indicates that he wasn't a property owner and/or didn't have sufficient personal goods to warrant his family undertaking the expense of a legal process.

REGISTERS

Registers are copy books made by the County Court Clerk, of probate grants and letters of administration. In the case of probate, a copy of the will is often included.

In Chapter 5, Section G, Deeds, we looked at General Registers from 1866 of the Land Registry Offices which contain unprobated wills that have no specific property description.

GUARDIANSHIP

Guardianship papers are a good source of family information, but official occurrences were not common before 1858. Since 1827, guardianship cases were included in Surrogate Court records and their indexes. These could tell you name of deceased parent, names and ages of children, and name of applicant for guardianship, often a relative.

It was rare for a father to apply for guardianship when his wife died, as he was considered to "own" the children. You will find that it's usually the widow or male relative of the deceased father who applies.

C) Surrogate Clerk's Application Books (AO)

APPLICATION BOOKS

With the sole establishment of the county Surrogate Court system, a central register was kept from 1859 of every application received in the province, whether for probate or administration. This system is a real boon for genealogists, in that the surname index covers the whole province, which is most valuable when date and place of death are unknown.

The *Index*, which is on microfilm at AO to 1967, will direct you to chronological Application Books, which are filmed to 1923. After that date, you can ask for the original Application Book. The entry here will tell you name of deceased, residence, date of death, name, occupation and residence of applicant, and in what county the probate/administration took place.

The next step leads to the relevant *County* Surrogate Court Index, already discussed above.

D) General Quarter Sessions of the Peace (AO)

QUARTER SESSIONS
District Courts of General Quarter Sessions of the Peace provided, in effect, local government up to 1841. Surviving records are at AO with finding aids listed both under "Court Records" and "Municipal Records".

Names of district officials appear here, along with anyone who became involved with administration of daily life or "disturbing the peace". For example, one would apply to the court for a licence to operate a tavern, or to perform marriages. There are roads reports, lands sold for tax arrears, registers of fines and forfeitures for wrongdoing.

The minute books of many courts have survived, which are really the key to their contents. Besides possibly finding an ancestor's name and establishing his residence at the time, you'll see some social background to the period. Look to the handy Finding Aid first.

Local newspapers always carried details of the court's proceedings. If an ancestor was involved in disturbing the peace or wrongdoing, you might then be able to find some colourful coverage of the story.

Other court records are held at AO and they will only be of interest to the occasional genealogist who might find a reference from some other source. Court records can be a veritable maze to most of us, so only those of most value in genealogy have been mentioned. We recommend the fine Inventory of Court Records at AO prepared by Catherine Shepard for any who want to pursue an esoteric legal reference.

TREASON
Prosecution of traitors to the Crown occurred most notably after the War of 1812 and the 1837 Rebellion. Records of such proceedings were kept according to the government agency involved.

At AO and PAC the Calendar to *Upper Canada Sundries* can lead into the Civil Secretary's correspondence and trials of 1812-1814 traitors. A *High*

Treason Register was compiled many years ago listing names alphabetically. In the above mentioned AO Inventory of Court Records, *Court of King's Bench* should be investigated for high treason records.

Not all traitors or rebels were summarily hanged; many disappeared quickly without being captured, leaving behind only witnesses' affidavits attesting to their treason. After the Rebellion of 1837, some rebels were sent to Australia for life; some were transported for shorter periods or banished from Ontario for life; lesser transgressors were pardoned on security of good behaviour. Upper Canada Sundries contain details of these hearings, contents of which are arranged chronologically.

Such records are not commonly used by genealogists as they haven't always been accessible, and would only apply to a small number of ancestors. Nevertheless they can give you a worthwhile and well-described insight into an ancestor's character and activities.

The judicial system and its courts and records were of course not set up for ancestor-hunters; beyond the main records mentioned here, one needs a detailed understanding of the system and its procedures. One introduction is "Court Records As a Genealogical Source" by Gordon Dodds, in *Readings in Ontario Genealogical Studies*.

District Courthouse and Gaol, Picton
Sketch by William Kettlewell
from *Ontario Historic Sites, Museums, Galleries and Plaques*

7/ Immigration/Naturalization

A) Ships' Lists
(PAC, AO)

Almost everyone wants to find their emigrating family on a ship's passenger list, tangible evidence that they did indeed endure that long and cruel voyage. It's unfortunate that most will be disappointed. Before 1865 there was no legal reason for Canadian officials or ship companies to keep nominal lists of arrivals here.

Some records that have turned up from the Colonial Office 1817-1831 are indexed by surname at PAC. A few others were mainly for subsidized emigration schemes like those of Peter Robinson or Lord Selkirk, which lists can be seen at AO and PAC.

Emigrant Agent's Offices were created in the 1820's and 1830's along the St. Lawrence River and the Great Lakes, to exercise some control over sick or indigent arrivals, and a few sources of genealogical value have survived from these "field offices". At PAC there is a card catalogue of arrivals who were provisioned by the agents in the 1840's. Almost nothing in the way of records remains for Ontario from the later quarantine stations.

After 1865 ships' lists are more common, at PAC on microfilm for the official ports of entry: *Quebec* from 1865, and *Halifax* from 1881. Both of these series extend on microfilm to about 1910. After 1900 other Canadian ports and some U.S. ports are included. Thousands of passengers arriving at either port had Ontario as their final destination. Some of the early years are indexed on cards at PAC. Otherwise, the films are arranged chronologically by year of arrival, with a list of the ships at the beginning of each year.

These lists vary in content a great deal, but the best will include all family members, ages, previous residence, and eventual destination. Conversion lists of the arrival years to 1900 and corresponding film numbers are in *The Canadian Genealogical Handbook*.

One point to remember is that depending on the time period and conditions in continental Europe, non-British emigrants usually went to a British port to transfer to a ship for Canada. In the earliest years few passenger ships arrived directly from continental Europe; this had changed dramatically by the end of the nineteenth century.

B) Naturalization
(PAC, AO)

NATURALIZATION

Naturalization, as a government policy, grew out of political concern about non-British immigrants and the matter of loyalty to the British Crown. Sensitivity on the issue was directly influenced by the arrival of U.S.-born settlers after the War of 1812. Before 1828 an Oath of Allegiance was a requirement in the land granting process, but there was no other formal requirement of citizenship or immigration.

Upper Canada Naturalization records from 1828 to 1850 are at PAC and consist of oaths or affirmations that the man had lived here for at least seven years and bore allegiance to the Crown. The law required this within seven to ten years of arrival as a means of ensuring serious intentions of permanent residency.

INDEXES

Donald McKenzie has prepared a nominal index to these volumes, published serially in *Families*, Vol. 18, No. 3 (1979), Vol. 19, Nos. 1-3 (1980), with a good introduction. The index will tell you name, file year, county or district of residence, and entry number. The actual register will give name, residence, occupation, signature, and date.

These registers apply only to *non-British* subjects. If your ancestor was born in England, Scotland, Ireland, or Wales, he was already a natural-born British subject.

After Confederation the federal government began to acquire responsibility for immigration through different Departments over the years. Naturalization records made by the Department of the Secretary of State from 1865-1917 were destroyed, but an index remains with some genealogical information. To use the index, you must know name, occupation, year of naturalization, and residence.

For naturalizations after 1917 the Citizenship Registration Branch of the Department of Secretary of State (address in Appendix I) has microfilm copies of the full records, accessible by name and date/place of birth. However, *only* the naturalized immigrant himself has access to these records, with a few exceptions. The status of being a Canadian Citizen as such did not begin until an Act of 1947.

Two articles in *Families*, Vol. 16, No. 4 (1977) are recommended: Bryan Corbett's "Genealogical Sources in the Historical Immigration Records" and Patricia Kennedy's "Records of the Immigration Process: Pre-Confederation".

C) Immigration
(AO)

The province of Ontario kept its own Department of Immigration after Confederation, the records of which are now at AO with a Finding Aid. For genealogical purposes, useful items might be Letterbooks 1869-1901 indexed by name, Destination Registers 1872-1874, Passage Warrants 1872-1888, and Applications for Refunds 1872-1875 indexed by name.

There is a group of early records on microfilm under the ambiguous title *"Emigrant Returns"* at AO for which the Finding Aid is filed under "Crown Lands". The Finding Aid lists surnames alphabetically. On the film itself is a description of contents, actually returns of Scottish and Irish settlers and disbanded regular army troops in the Lanark County area, between 1815 and 1834. These include the military settlements at Lanark, Perth, and Richmond.

Many of these returns give property descriptions for the settler, indicating his date of arrival. For example, there is a list of ex-military settlers eligible for patents in 1822 and a list of Lanark settlers who received government "stores" or supplies 1821-1828.

D) Oaths of Allegiance

In the beginning these were part of everyone's application for a Crown land grant, therefore many are still found in documentation of Upper Canada Land Petitions (PAC, AO). Some are also found in the Township Papers Series (AO) and in Heir and Devisee Commission records.

The Baldwin Room at the Metropolitan Toronto Reference Library also has a collection. These were published by Marion Keffer in *York Pioneer* in issues of 1961 and 1963. Names of settlers are given, as are previous residence, current residence, and an identifying physical description.

THE PETER ROBINSON EMIGRANTS
From the Peter Robinson Papers — 1825

Irish Emigrants on Board the *John Barry* — 1825

(Courtesy Archives of Ontario.)

8/ Municipal Records
(AO, Municipalities)

The Municipal Act of 1850 put local government in the hands of elected town or township officials. Prior to this, local judicial and municipal business was handled by District Councils 1842-1849, and earlier by the District Courts of Quarter Sessions (see Chapter 6, Court Records, Section D).

In 1850 County Councils "replaced" District Councils although the judicial aspect was removed. At AO a detailed inventory of municipal records with appendices will lead you to your geographic location.

District Council records include, as well as meeting minutes, correspondence, and bylaws, some school papers, roads and bridges reports, poll books, and land registers. These are arranged by district name.

County Council records are arranged by county name and include minutes, account books, committee reports, bylaws, some militia rolls, and assessment records.

ASSESSMENT, COLLECTORS' ROLLS

Township/Town Council records are arranged alphabetically in the inventory by the appropriate county name. Included here are the usual minutes and proceedings, tax collectors' rolls, assessment rolls, and poll books. Generally there are few assessment and collectors' rolls pre-1850, although Council minutes often pre-date the Municipal Act.

VOTERS' LISTS

Voters' lists were kept from 1867 for years when an election was held. Assessments, collectors' rolls, and voters' lists vary in information from property description to personal property, but serve to locate an ancestor at a specific date and time.

LOCAL CENSUS

The occasional pre-1842 census return is found, listed in the AO inventory and in the *Index to Census of Canada (Ontario)*. These are only for townships in parts of the Counties of Leeds and Grenville, Lanark, Carleton, Northumberland and Durham, Victoria, Peterborough, Prescott and Russell.

9/ Education Records
(AO)

Don't expect to find a lot of lists with pupils' names here. This extensive collection is divided into a *government records* section and a *private manuscripts* section. The first includes the provincial Department of Education records of meeting minutes, correspondence, laws, inspectors' and trustees' reports, local Board of Education minutes, teachers' contracts and training records.

Volume Two of the Finding Aid is 143 pages of description including some local school histories and teaching experiences, with files for each teaching subject. Important here for a teacher-ancestor are the *Superannuation Applications* by teachers, listed nominally 1852-1912.

Records of county Boards of Education circa 1850-1910 contain some students' examination results and registers (elementary school, high school, separate school) but many are subject to the 100-year restriction to access.

The private manuscripts section is in chronological arrangement, consisting of correspondence, legal papers, land transactions, insurance and building maintenance for schools, teacher/trustee agreements, certificates, pamphlets, administration files, etc.

To get something useful from these records it's necessary to spend enough time examining the Finding Aid and relating the locations and dates to your family.

PORT ARTHUR PUBLIC SCHOOLS

Certificate of Promotion

This Certifies that *Clara Freiberg*

has completed the Course of Study prescribed for the *Sr. VIII* Class and that *her* Deportment has been such that *she* is entitled to *Special Hon.* Promotion

to the *Jr. IX* Class, having obtained a Standing of *89* per cent.

Port Arthur, June 29th, 192 *6*

Wm. J. Jard Principal   *S. T. Watson* Teacher

10/ Military and Naval Records

The Militia Act of 1855 for the first time established a paid peace-time militia of Canadians, called the "active militia", the forerunner of the Canadian Armed Forces. Before this, defense of Ontario and other provinces was provided by regular British Army troops.

MILITIA

The local militia system existed from earliest times, but apart from participation in the War of 1812 and the Rebellion of 1837 their activity seems to have been limited to the annual muster for training. Able-bodied men between the ages of 16 and 60 were required to serve in a militia unit, often referred to as the "sedentary militia", usually organized on a county basis.

In 1866 the Active Militia saw their first battle action during the Fenian Raids. Canadian Army contingents later took part in South Africa's Boer War and the two World Wars.

Muster rolls of militia units have survived for scattered counties and dates, indicating a man's name with sometimes age and home township. None of them are found in one central collection. At AO they may be catalogued under "militia" or "military" or by county holdings. At PAC, enrollment lists, muster rolls, and pay lists for militia are found in various records groups according to the government or military department responsible for them at that time.

To understand and locate different types of military and defense records we suggest reading "Military and Naval Records" in PAC's *Tracing Your Ancestors in Canada*; "An Introduction to Military Records for the Genealogist" by Eric Jonasson in *Families*, Vol. 20, No. 4 (1981); and *Searching for a Soldier in the British Army or Canadian Militia* by John H. Grenville.

NAVAL

The Provincial Marine and the Admiralty Lake Service records are at PAC, actually contained within the grouping of Office of the Commander of the Forces, British North America.

BRITISH ARMY

Much of the British Army records relating to Canada are at the War Office collection, Public Record Office, at Kew, Richmond, England. Details of an individual's service record are more numerous for officers than for enlisted men. It is essential that you know the name of your ancestor's regiment to begin any research. Some War Office records are available on microfilm from the LDS Library, once you've determined from their catalogue which film to order.

Copies of War Office records at PAC include muster rolls for Canadian Militia and Volunteers 1837-1850 on microfilm. There is an incomplete nominal card index to PAC's massive Military "C" Series, records of British forces in Canada. PAC also has some filmed monthly returns of officers, arranged by regiment, in MG 13.

If your ancestor first came to Canada or Ontario with the British Army, a regimental history will be useful for learning postings of the different battalions. Arthur White's *A Bibliography of Regimental Histories of the British Army* can help with a book title. The Royal Canadian Military Institute in Toronto has an extensive library of military subjects.

Eric Jonasson has published *Canadian Veterans of the War of 1812* with a considerable introduction to the records of this War, but it should be noted that the list of veterans derives from a list *only of veterans still living 1875-1877*.

Perseverance in searching for genealogical, social, or historical aspects of military life so many years ago can result in finding such records as "Militia General Courts Martial" in *Appendix to the Journal of the House of Assembly of Upper Canada: Session 1839*.

MEDALS

Other records relating to the military and militia are Medal Registers for the War of 1812, Fenian raids, and South African War, at PAC with a microfilm index 1866-1902 that includes the War of 1812 Registers.

CLAIMS

Claims for losses during war activities are mentioned here only briefly. After the American Revolution, a British Claims Commission received applications for compensation of losses suffered by Loyalists. Because of the war with Britain, Loyalists lost property and possessions. This will be discussed in Chapter 11 on Loyalist Sources.

During the War of 1812 and the Rebellion of 1837 some civilians had property destroyed by invading forces, or goods seized by the defenders to supply the fighting troops. At PAC you can find Claims for Losses for both these periods. At AO some of these may be found in manuscript material catalogued under county names, e.g. Hastings (County) Rebellion Claims 1837-1845.

CHELSEA PENSIONERS

Many British soldiers who spent time in Canada during their service, returned to settle here after being discharged. Some wounded soldiers who were pensioned out of the Army after spending time in Chelsea Hospital, London, eventually came to Ontario. In *Families*, Vol. 23, Nos. 3 & 4 (1984) Barbara Aitken has compiled lists of these men from Colonial Office and War Office documents, with as much information on each as is available from the original records.

TWENTIETH CENTURY WARS

For reading about the *South Africa* or "Boer" War, consult *Families*, Vol. 21, No. 1 (1982). In "Serving the Empire: Canadians in South Africa, 1899-1902" Glenn Wright describes the considerable number of records available on these service men at PAC. To all intents and purposes, personal records from *World Wars I and II* are closed files. Personnel files are at the Federal Department of Veterans Affairs. Some information in a particular circumstance *might* be released to the veteran himself or a next of kin, but don't count on this as a genealogical source.

"Military Sources at the Public Archives of Canada" by Carl A. Christie in *Families*, Vol. 16, No. 4 (1977) is another more detailed article.

Illustration called "The Lost Chief" from *Mr. Punch's History of the Great War*

11/ Loyalist Sources
(PAC, AO)

Loyalist records as such are not a separate group of documents. Evidence of Loyalist ancestry is found in the usual documentation processes for any ancestor, such as land records or military papers, but the Loyalists arrived in Ontario before other settlers. The term "Loyalist" is used here as the popular expression of the designation *UE*. It refers to the person entitled by government recognition to the use of the initials "U.E." (Unity of Empire) because of his adherence to the Crown during the American Revolution and subsequent removal to Canada.

Basically, a Loyalist was a person who resided in the American Colonies before the war with Britain, who joined the British forces in some capacity, and who experienced some loss of property, goods, or life. Some widows of men who died in the British cause received land grants that recognized the men as Loyalists.

LOYALIST LISTS

The Loyalists who came to this newly created province were given a free land grant, the size of which was commensurate with regimental rank. From 1796 a list was kept by two different government offices so that true Loyalists could receive this privilege, and unqualified persons could be excluded. The result was two lists which didn't entirely coincide.

Many settlers arriving later than the end of the war in 1783 were claiming UE benefits. The Executive Council UE List is the more accurate source (PAC: RG1, L7, Vol 52A) consisting of some 3,000 names; it was constantly being updated with insertions and removals, right into the 1850's. Excluded were military claimants, children of UE's, and regular soldiers and seamen.

Generation Press expects to publish the *Executive List of U.E. Loyalists* in 1985, with a lengthy introduction and explanation. It shows the man's name and District of settlement. Note that Reid's *The Loyalists in Ontario* is a guide only; all children may not be listed if some failed to apply for a land grant or to confirm their father's status.

The "Old" UE List of the Crown Lands Department has about 6,000 names, with only about one half of those "true" Loyalists. Nevertheless this is still a good source for early settlers, found at both PAC and AO.

Loyalist Claims for Losses, perhaps the only "real" records created for this group, were heard by a British government Commission which convened at various cities in Canada and in London, England (PAC: MG 12 & 13; AO: *1904 Bureau of Archives Report*). A researcher can find details of an individual's residence and possessions before 1776, length of residence in the States, occupation, dependants, if and when he joined the Royal Standard as a fighting man, his location in 1783 and/or residence as of the date of the claim.

Once again, not all Loyalists made application to the Commission, for various reasons, mostly a matter of distance or expenditure. Some applied through an agent such as *John Porteous* or *Alexander Ellice* (their Papers at PAC: MG 23 & 24). Also not everyone who applied for compensation was deemed a Loyalist.

Claims to the Commission in Audit Office Series 13, Bundles 1-35 & 37 have been summarized in Coldham's book *American Loyalist Claims Vol. 1* (Appendix II), alphabetically by surname.

Muster rolls of the Loyalist Corps (the term "corps" is similar to the army "regiment") were taken at different times from the formation of a corps until the end of the Revolution when they were disbanded. For our purposes, those who later settled in Ontario were disbanded around the Montreal area.

Some of these original lists have been found and many have been published. Originals at PAC are in RG 8 Series 1, indexed, and in Haldimand Papers MG 21, unindexed, the latter among a great deal of other related material. E. Keith Fitzgerald has prepared lists of over 2,000 Loyalist names and families from several sources in the Haldimand Papers, which OGS is issuing as an individual publication.

Rolls of the Provincial (Loyalist) Corps, Canadian Command, American Revolutionary Period by Mary Beacock Fryer and Lt.-Col. William A. Smy is a consolidation of many lists. The authors have chosen lists of some major corps at the most complete size of each, which range from 1781-1784. Not all corps are shown in this book, and information on each man varies from nothing other than name, to birthplace (N.B. means North Britain), age, length of service, and height. If previous residence isn't given, you can get closer to the truth about your man with some research on where his corps was raised. It could happen that your ancestor wasn't on the particular list you see. If you think or know he did

That he did many services to Govert. in the course of the war. That he had good Improvts on some Lands belonging to Mr. John Jones near Fort Edward. That he had 4 or 5 Milch Cows, 2 good Mares, and had a good House, comfortably furnished, which was burnt by the Rebels.

A New Claim.

Montreal,
26th January,
1788.

318. Evidence on the Claim of DANIEL ROBERTSON, late of Albany County.

WM. FERGUSON, Father in Law to Claimt., Sworn:

Says that Daniel Robertson lost his life in 1786 by an accident. From the information he has had he was in 1783 at—

He was a native of Scotland, and came to America in 1774.

He was a Loyal Man, and came to Canada in 1776, and was a Sergt. in McAlpine's Corps. He had been in Capt. McAlpine's family.

(50).

He has left 2 Infant Children who are supported by Wits. at New Johnston.

The Claim is for Clothes Lost at the Convention, which Wits. believes was the case.

A New Claim.

Montreal,
26th January,
1788.

319. Evidence on the Claim of JEAN SUTHERLAND, late of Cherry Valley, N. York Province.

Claimt. Sworn:

Received for
the children.

Says she lived in Montreal 1783, and had 2 Infant Children of Hector Sutherlands with her, viz., William, 13 years old, in the States. Catharine, 10 years old, with Wits.

Her late Husband, Hector Sutherlard, came from Scotland in 1773, & was settled at Cherry Valley on the Susquehana.

He was put in gaol in 1777 & the year following came to Niagara where he died. He was a soldier in Butler's Rangers.

He had 100 acres, 6 of which were cleared. Says it was on a Lease for ever from a Campbell, a rebel. He had built a House & Barn. They had 3 Milch Cows, a Horse and 2 Sheep. Some Furniture. They were taken by the Rebels

(51).

Affidavit DOND. MCDONELL that her husband was a Loyal Man and Lost his all.

A New Claim.

Montreal,
28th January,
1788.

320. Evidence on the Claim of ALEXR. MCDONELL, late of Tryon County, N.Y. Province.

JOHN MCDONELL, oldest son of Claimt. Sworn:

Says his Father was at Macheche in 1783.

A sample of Claims for Losses from *Bureau of Archives Report, 1904.*

47

military service you may have to search out other lists taken at different periods.

Also recommended is Fryer's companion volume, *King's Men, The Soldier Founders of Ontario.*

Other sources for information on Loyalist ancestors are those previously discussed under the Land Records heading, especially Upper Canada Land Petitions and the Heir and Devisee Commission records. Any records group of data sources for early settlers will also apply to UE's.

PETITIONS

Children of a UE were also entitled to a free 100 acre land grant, although not all petitioned for it. This was their right when they reached the age of 21, often a helpful clue to ages. Daughters often applied after their marriage. Some were not approved for grants, for lack of evidence that the father was a genuine UE. Whereas the UE himself would give some evidence in his petition for his claim, such as military service, his son or daughter would petition identifying the UE father with some character references to prove it. Some petitions of sons and daughters were not "approved" for their fathers were not deemed UE for insufficient evidence of military service, etc. In the case of a daughter, she usually gives her husband's name as well as her father's.

PUBLISHED SOURCES

Reid's original book, which was compiled basically from the Orders-in-Council issued to UE children, has recently been re-published as *The Loyalists in Ontario: The Sons and Daughters of the American Loyalists of Upper Canada* by Hunterdon House. Added to Mr. Reid's compendium of families is a welcome index to all "stray" names. The book should be treated as the secondary source it is, and not regarded as definitive or conclusive with regard to family structure and extra information from other sources, but it can provide valuable leads to family locations, names, and primary source material.

Audrey and Robert Kirk's presentation "Approaches to U.E. Loyalist Research" in *Readings in Ontario Genealogical Sources* gives more background on UE history and sources. We have mentioned other publications earlier in the text. See also the excellent References bibliography for "Loyalists" in *Some Ontario References and Sources for the Family Historian.*

Norman Crowder relates the steps he followed in tracing his own ancestry in "More About the Loyalists in Ontario" in *Families*, Vol. 23, No. 3 (1984).

The United Empire Loyalist Association of Canada is firstly a membership of UE descendants who must prove their pedigrees to be called UE today. Applications are processed by a local and by the Dominion genealogist. Other degrees of membership are offered.

The Toronto Branch of the Association published, as their Bicentennial project in 1984, *Loyalist Lineages of Canada 1783-1983*, which contains all the pedigrees received to 1983.

The 1984 OGS Seminar was planned on the Loyalist Bicentennial theme and the *Seminar Annual* contains articles on families and groups who were part of this migration.

St. Andrew's Presbyterian Church, Williamstown, Glengarry County, Congregation formed in 1787
Sketch by William Kettlewell from *Ontario Historic Sites, Museums, Galleries and Plaques*

The "do-it-yourself" genealogist isn't totally blocked when a visit to a local Ontario resource centre isn't possible for personal examination of records material. The public library in your home town may have more than you think. You might ask if they can acquire some of the more general publications. A university library, if accessible, collects historical material relevant to the courses it offers. A local genealogical or historical society may be on a subscription exchange with OGS; again, you might enquire if this is a feasible request.

CORRESPONDENCE

Writing letters is the genealogist's lot when records aren't accessible. Remember that U.S. stamps can't be used in Canada. If you're American, ask your local genealogical society how to obtain Canadian stamps. Genealogical societies with international members usually have people who will purchase stamps of their own country for other members. Otherwise an International Postal Reply Coupon should be sent with every letter, and always a self-addressed envelope. This enclosure can speed up response and establish an important sense of good will.

Requesting a search from the register of a local church, a place that doesn't employ staff for this purpose, is better received if a token money order is enclosed. We suggest a minimum of $5, or more, depending on how much you ask for. One professional researcher's practice is to offer the money order for the time spent by someone to search the registers; if the volunteer searcher should refuse the money, the professional makes it clear that it should be used as a church donation.

Unfortunately there will always be a small percentage who won't reply no matter how nice or how desperate you sound. Always be concise and as brief as possible.

Writing to a church archives should obtain for you the address of an individual church, if you supplied a place-name. You may or may not be told that the registers you seek are in their holdings, according to their policy and staff time. For instance, the PCA (see Appendix I for addresses) will try to accommodate written requests from such a distance that precludes a personal visit. The UCA can't do this, but will send a list of professional researchers.

Both the PAC and AO will answer limited queries but we urge that you not abuse the system. Cutbacks in government spending and staff in these public institutions could possibly reduce this practice. Both will also supply lists of local researchers familiar with their holdings.

INTERLIBRARY LOAN

Many records that have been microfilmed are available through Interlibrary Loan anywhere in the U.S. or Canada from the PAC. The requirement is that your local library belong to the system and have a microfilm reader. Films are loaned to a library (*not to an individual!*) for a small charge to cover postage.

So the good news is that just about everything at *PAC* mentioned in this text as "microfilmed" can be read by you in your home town library. You may have to write PAC first to obtain the film numbers, such as those for census or church registers, for ordering at your library.

The bad news is that *AO* does not participate in Interlibrary Loan. Records unique to AO are available only on site.

You'll find that most smaller local libraries, museums, and archives will generally respond to a written query, although many have only part-time hours and staff.

LDS LIBRARY

Another Library is that of the Church of Jesus Christ of Latter Day Saints, more popularly known as Mormons. It's known as the LDS Library among genealogists. It is a requirement of their faith that Mormons trace their ancestry, and by collecting copies of genealogical records from all over the world, the LDS Church has made it easier for members to do this. The main LDS Library in Salt Lake City contains the world's largest collection of genealogical records. Of course these are not all Mormon records; Mormon ancestry goes back beyond its relatively recent beginnings to roots in other countries and religions.

Microfilm copies of anything in their holdings can be sent to one of their Branch Libraries from Salt Lake City for a small loan and postage charge. Non-LDS Church members are welcome to use the facilities of a Branch or the main Library. The staff at the Branch Libraries are volunteer Church members who will help you to find appropriate catalogues, inventories, etc. for ordering a microfilm, but they cannot undertake research for you.

Their holdings for Ontario are growing all the time, and include the Deeds, Deeds Indexes, Abstract Indexes, CLRI, some Surrogate Court Indexes, some collectors' and assessment rolls, and a variety of church registers. Not all cities in Canada and the U.S. and not all Mormon churches have a Branch Library. (See *Some Ontario References and Sources for the Family Historian* for LDS Branch Library addresses in Ontario.)

For those readers unfamiliar with the LDS Library collection, David Pratt has an article for beginners in *Families* Vol. 20, No. 4 (1981): "Using the IGI to Solve Research Problems".

HIRED
RESEARCHERS

If you receive a list of professional researchers from some institution, it won't recommend any one person above another. It's to your benefit to query two or more to reach a satisfactory agreement. Fees vary, and may range from an hourly rate to specific search charges. There is a growing number of resident Ontario genealogists who are experienced in the records of these major institutions, and in smaller local collections. See "Wanted: Hired Genealogist" in *Canadian Genealogist*, Vol. 4, No. 1 (1982) by Brenda Merriman.

QUERIES

Inserting queries in OGS *Families* was already mentioned as a way to contact others of mutual research interest. When a contact is made, it often saves research time, frustration, and duplication of effort. An offer to exchange information is basic courtesy. Joining an OGS Branch also opens up new doors to source material.

Appendix I: Resource Centres

A) Major Repositories and References

PAC   Public Archives of Canada   (...Manuscript Division
395 Wellington Street   ...Public Records Division
Ottawa, Ontario   ...etc)
K1A 0N3

AO   Archives of Ontario
77 Grenville Street
Toronto, Ontario
M7A 2R9

RGO   Office of the Registrar General
MacDonald Block
Queen's Park
Toronto, Ontario
M7A 1Y5

     OGS Library
North York Public Library
35 Fairview Mall Drive
Willowdale, Ontario

MTL   Metropolitan Toronto   (...Canadian History
    Central Library   ...Baldwin Room)
789 Yonge Street
Toronto, Ontario
M4W 2G8

NLC   National Library of Canada
395 Wellington Street
Ottawa, Ontario
K1A 0N4

     Official Documents Section   (Copies of Patents)
Ministry of Government Services
Hearst Block, 3rd Floor
Queen's Park
Toronto, Ontario
M7A 1N3

     Ministry of Natural   (Current Patent Index)
    Resources
Land Management Branch
Titles Section, Room 6621
Whitney Block
Queen's Park
Toronto, Ontario
M7A 1W3

     Clerk of the Senate
Parliament Buildings
Ottawa, Ontario
K1A 0A4

Citizenship Registration Branch
Department of the Secretary of State
15 Eddy Street
Hull, Quebec
K1A 0M5

Voluntary Adoption Disclosure Registry
700 Bay Street, 2nd Floor
Toronto, Ontario
M7A 1E9

UCA

United Church of Canada Archives
Victoria University
73 Queen's Park Crescent East
Toronto, Ontario
M5S 1K7

PCA

Presbyterian Church in Canada Archives
Knox College
59 St. George Street
Toronto, Ontario
M5S 2E6

CBA

Canadian Baptist Archives
McMaster Divinity College
McMaster University
Hamilton, Ontario
L8S 4K1

Canadian Jewish Congress
Central Region Archives
150 Beverley Street
Toronto, Ontario
M5T 1Y6

Mennonite Archives of Ontario
Conrad Grebel College
University of Waterloo
Waterloo, Ontario
N2L 3G1

Lutheran Church in America
Eastern Canada Synod Archives
Wilfrid Laurier University
Waterloo, Ontario
N2L 3C5

Royal Canadian Military Institute
426 University Avenue
Toronto, Ontario
M5G 1S9

Canadian Society of Friends (Quaker)
60 Lowther Avenue
Toronto, Ontario
M5R 1C7

Local and University Libraries:

See *Canadian Almanac and Directory* (see full listing in Appendix II) and also "Library Information" in *Some Ontario References and Sources for the Family Historian.*

B) Associations, many with Periodicals & Publications

OGS
Ontario Genealogical Society
P.O. Box 66, Station Q
Toronto, Ontario
M4T 2L7

UEL
United Empire Loyalists' Association of Canada
Dominion Headquarters
23 Prince Arthur Avenue
Toronto, Ontario
M5R 1B2

OHS
Ontario Historical Society
78 Dunloe Road, Room 207
Toronto, Ontario
M5P 2T6

Pennsylvania German Folklore Society of Canada
c/o 106 Maplewood Place
Kitchener, Ontario
N2H 4L5

Huguenot Society of Canada
Box 1003, Station A
Toronto, Ontario
M5W 1G5

The Heraldry Society of Canada
125 Lakeway Drive
Ottawa, Ontario
K1L 5A9

The Multicultural History Society of Ontario
43 Queen's Park Crescent East
Toronto, Ontario
M5S 2C3

Centre de Recherche en Civilisation
    Canadienne-Francaise
Universite d'Ottawa
65, rue Hastey
Ottawa, Ontario
K1N 6N5

Legislative Library of Ontario
Parliament Buildings
Queen's Park
Toronto, Ontario
M7A 1A2

Appendix II: Publications

A) Publishers and Book Sellers
(ask for lists/catalogues)

Ontario Genealogical Society
P.O. Box 66, Station Q
Toronto, Ontario
M4T 2L7

Generation Press
172 King Henrys Boulevard
Agincourt, Ontario
M1T 2V6

Wheatfield Press
Box 205, St. James Postal Station
Winnipeg, Manitoba
R3J 3R4

Mika Publishing Company
P.O. Box 536
Belleville, Ontario
K8N 5B2

Dundurn Press Limited
P.O. Box 245, Station F
Toronto, Ontario
M4Y 2L5

Hunterdon House
38 Swan Street
Lambertville, NJ 08530
U.S.A.

The Bookcellar
144 James Street South
Hamilton, Ontario
L8P 3A2

The Highway Book Shop
Cobalt, Ontario
P0J 1C0

Government Publication Centre (PAC
Supply and Services   Publications)
Hull, Quebec K1A 0S9

Ontario Government Bookstore
880 Bay Street
Toronto, Ontario
M7A 2R9

Cumming Publishers   (County Atlases)
Box 23
Stratford, Ontario
N5A 6S8

Huronia-Canadiana Books
Box 685
Alliston, Ontario
L0M 1A0

B) Maps

Ministry of Transportation & Communications
1201 Wilson Avenue
Downsview, Ontario
M3M 1J8

Perly's Variprint Limited
1050 Eglinton Avenue West
Toronto, Ontario
M6C 2C5

Generation Press
172 King Henrys Boulevard
Agincourt, Ontario
M1T 2V6

Cluny Press
Box 2207
Kingston, Ontario
K7L 5J9

C) Serial Publications

See lists of addresses in Appendix I for "Associations".

Newspapers are of prime interest to the genealogist and the family historian. Ontario's first newspaper, the *Upper Canada Gazette* (also known as the *American Oracle*), was first published at Niagara in 1792. AO and NLC have extensive collections for hundreds of Ontario towns. You are advised to locate the nearest town to your ancestor's home. Nineteenth century newspapers for that town, which usually include news from surrounding townships and rural areas, may be in the AO collection which is largely microfilmed.

Directories are another type of intermittent publication used by genealogists, and will be found in most local libraries from the present time back to varying dates. Please see reference to local libraries and archives in Appendix I.

Ryder, Dorothy E., *Checklist of Canadian Directories, 1790-1850*. Ottawa: National Library of Canada, 1979.

Canadian Genealogist, Generation Press, 172 King Henrys Boulevard, Agincourt, Ontario M1T 2V6.

Families, Ontario Genealogical Society, Box 66, Station Q, Toronto, Ontario M4T 2L7.

Lost in Canada? Joy Reisinger, Editor, 1020 Central Avenue, Sparta, WI 54656.

The Ontario Register, Thomas B. Wilson, Editor, 38 Swan Street, Lambertville, NJ 08530.

D) Selected Important Books: General Interest

Aitken, Barbara, Dawn Broughton, and Yvonne Crouch, *Some Ontario References and Sources for the Family Historian*. Toronto: OGS 1984.

Allen, Robert S., *Loyalist Literature, An Annotated Bibliographic Guide to the Writings on the Loyalists of the American Revolution*. Toronto: Dundurn Press, 1982.

Baxter, Angus, *In Search of Your Roots*. Toronto: Macmillan Company, 1978.

Beddoe, Lt. Cdr. Alan, *Beddoe's Canadian Heraldry*. Rev. by Col. Strome Galloway. Belleville: Mika Publishing, no date.

Birkett, Patricia, Janine Roy, and Lorraine St.-Louis, *Checklist of Parish Registers 1981*. Ottawa: PAC, 1981.

Bureau of Archives, Second Report. Toronto: Province of Ontario, 1904.

Canadian Almanac and Directory. Toronto: Copp Clark, 1983.

Chadwick, Edward M., *Ontario Families: Genealogies of United Empire Loyalist and Other Pioneer Families of Upper Canada*. (1894) Reprint Belleville: Mika Publishing, 1972.

Coderre, John, *Searching in the Public Archives*. Ottawa Branch OGS, 1972.

Coldham, Peter W., *American Loyalist Claims, Vol I*. Washington, DC: National Genealogical Society, 1980.

Craig, Gerald, *Upper Canada: The Formative Years, 1784-1841*. Toronto: McClelland and Stewart, 1963.

Directory of Canadian Archives. Ottawa: Bureau of Canadian Archivists and Association of Canadian Archivists, 1981.

Directory of Surnames, 1984 Edition. Toronto: OGS, 1984.

Doane, Gilbert, *Searching For Your Ancestors*. New York: Bantam Books, 1974.

Fryer, Mary B., *King's Men, The Soldier Founders of Ontario*. Toronto: Dundurn Press, 1980.

Fryer, Mary B., and Lt. Col. William A. Smy, *Rolls of the Provincial (Loyalist) Corps, Canadian Command, American Revolutionary Period*. Toronto: Dundurn Press, 1981.

Gates, Lillian F., *Land Policies of Upper Canada*. Toronto: University of Toronto Press, 1968.

Genealogical Sources, Archives of Ontario. Toronto: AO, 1981.

General Guide Series. Ottawa: PAC 1983 and 1984. Guides have been published for the Federal Archives Division and for the Archives Library. Guides to the other PAC Divisions should be completed by fall of 1984. All PAC publications are available from "Government Publications Centre" above in A) Publishers and Book Sellers.

General Inventory of Manuscripts, Vol 3, MG 17- MG 21. Ottawa: PAC, 1974. *Vol 4, MG 22-25*, 1972.

Grenville, John H., *Searching For a Soldier in the British Army or Canadian Militia*. Kingston Branch OGS, 1977.

Harland, Derek, *Genealogical Research Standards*. Salt Lake City: Bookcraft, 1963.

Inventory of Recorded Cemeteries in Ontario, 1983. Toronto: OGS, 1983.

Jonasson, Eric, *The Canadian Genealogical Handbook*. Winnipeg: Wheatfield Press, 1978.

―――, *Canadian Veterans of the War of 1812*. Winnipeg: Wheatfield Press, 1981.

―――, *Untangling the Tree: Organizational Systems for the Family Historian*. Winnipeg: Wheatfield Press, 1983.

Kennedy, Patricia, *How to Trace Your Loyalist Ancestors*. Ottawa Branch OGS, 1972.

Kennedy, Patricia, and Janine Roy, *Tracing Your Ancestors in Canada*. Ottawa: PAC, 1983.

Lackey, Richard S., *Cite Your Sources*. New Orleans: Polyanthos, 1980.

Loyalist Lineages of Canada 1783-1983. Toronto Branch, United Empire Loyalist Association, 1984.

McFall, David and Jean, *Land Records in Ontario Registry Offices.* Toronto: OGS, 1984.

McKenzie, Donald A., *Death Notices from the Christian Guardian 1836-1850.* Lambertville, NJ: Hunterdon House, 1982.

Mika, Nick and Helma, *Places in Ontario, Their Names, Origins, and History. Part 1, A-E; Part 2, F-M; Part 3, N-Z.* Belleville: Mika Publishing, 1977, 1981, 1983.

Ontario Historic Sites, Museums, Galleries and Plaques. Toronto: Ministry of Culture and Recreation, Heritage Conservation Division.

Reid, William D., *Death Notices of Ontario.* Lambertville, NJ: Hunterdon House, 1980.

_____, *The Loyalists in Ontario, The Sons and Daughters of American Loyalists of Upper Canada.* Lambertville, NJ: Hunterdon House, 1973.

_____, *Marriage Notices of Ontario.* Lambertville, NJ: Hunterdon House, 1980.

Rubincam, Milton, Editor, *Genealogical Research: Methods and Sources, Vol I.* Washington, DC: American Society of Genealogists, 1980.

Smith, W.H., *Canadian Gazetteer.* (1846) Reprint Toronto: Coles Publishing Company, 1972.

Stevenson, Noel C., *Genealogical Evidence.* Laguna Hills, CA: Aegean Park Press, 1979.

_____, *Search and Research: The Researcher's Handbook.* Salt Lake City: Deseret Book Co., 1964.

Union List of Manuscripts in Canadian Repositories. Ottawa: PAC, 1975. (Annual supplements)

Wilson, Don, Compiler, *Readings in Ontario Genealogical Sources.* Toronto: Conference on Ontario Genealogical Sources, 1979.

Wilson, Thomas B., *Ontario Marriage Notices.* Lambertville, NJ: Hunterdon House, 1982.

Wright, Norman E., and David Pratt, *Genealogical Research Essentials.* Salt Lake City: Bookcraft Inc., 1967.

E) Selected Important Books: Local Research Aids

Aitken, Barbara B., *Local Histories of Ontario Municipalities, 1951-1977: A Bibliography.* Toronto: Ontario Library Association, 1978.

Anderson, Allan J., *Diocese of Ontario (Anglican Church of Canada) Archives: Preliminary Inventory, 1980.* Kingston: 1980.

Beattie, Judith, "Genealogical Sources in the Hudson's Bay Company Archives, Provincial Archives of Manitoba", *Seminar Annual, Sudbury 1983.* Toronto: OGS, 1983.

Blackburn, Helen, and Diane French, Judith Mitton, Jean Zimmer, Carol Marcelle, *Tracing Your Family in Kent County, A Guide for Beginners and Experts.* Kent County Branch OGS, n.d.

Bonk, Darryl, *How to Trace Your Family in Oxford County.* Oxford County Branch OGS, 1981.

Byerly, A.E., *The Beginning of Things in Wellington and Waterloo Counties.* 1935. Reprint 1982.

Canniff, William, *The Settlement of Upper Canada, with Specific Reference to the Bay of Quinte.* Toronto: 1869. Reprint Belleville, Mika Publishing, 1971.

Coleman, Thelma, *The Canada Company.* Stratford: County of Perth, Perth County Historical Board, and Cumming Publishers, 1978.

County Marriage Registers of Ontario, Canada, 1858-1869, Vol 1-15. Agincourt: Generation Press.

DeMarce, Virginia, *German Military Settlers in Canada, After the American Revolution.* Sparta, WI: Joy Reisinger, 1984.

Dorland, Arthur G., *The Quakers in Canada.* Toronto: Canadian Friends Historical Association, 1968.

Elford, Jean T., *History of Lambton County*. Sarnia: Lambton County Historical Society, 1969.

Elliott, Bruce S., *Tracing Your Ottawa Family*. Ottawa: Corporation of the City of Ottawa, 1980.

Epp, Frank, *Mennonites in Canada 1786-1920: The History of a Separate People*. Toronto: Macmillan, 1969.

Ermatinger, Edward, *Life of Colonel Talbot and the Talbot Settlement*. St. Thomas, 1859. Reprint Belleville: Mika Publishing, 1972.

Files, Angela, *Tracing Your Family in Brant County*. Mercantile Press, n.d.

Herrington, Walter S., *History of the County of Lennox and Addington*. Toronto, 1913. Reprint Belleville: Mika Publishing, 1972.

History of the County of Welland. Welland, 1887. Reprint Belleville: Mika Publishing, 1972.

Johnson, Leo A., *History of the County of Ontario, 1615-1875*. Whitby: Corporation of the County of Ontario, 1973.

Kirby, William, *Annals of Niagara*. Welland, 1896. Reprint Belleville: Mika Publishing, 1972.

Leavitt, Thaddeus, *History of Leeds and Grenville*, 1879. Reprint Belleville: Mika Publishing, 1975.

Mann, Trudy, and Jan Speers, *People of Peel, Indexes to Genealogical Source Material*. Mississauga: Mann & Speers, 1981.

_____, *Research in Halton and Peel: A Genealogical Handbook*. Oakville: Halton Peel Branch OGS, 1980.

McGill, Jean S., *A Pioneer History of the County of Lanark*. Bewdley: Clay Publishing Co., 1968.

Ontario's Heritage, A Guide to Archival Resources, Vol 1 (Peterborough Region), Vol 7 (Peel Region), Vol 12 (North-East Ontario). Cheltenham: Boston Mills Press, 1978-1980.

Owen, E.A., *Pioneer Sketches of Long Point Settlement*. Toronto, 1898. Reprint Belleville: Mika Publishing, 1972.

Paquette, Lisa, and Jack Ramieri, Jenny Varga, Compilers, *How To Trace Your Roots in Essex County: A Source Guide*. Windsor: Windsor Public Library, 1984.

Powell, Janet, *Annals of the Forty, Vol 1-10*. Grimsby: Grimsby Historical Society, 1950-1959.

Pringle, Jacob, *Lunenburgh or the Old Eastern District*. Cornwall: 1890. Reprint Belleville: Mika Publishing, 1980.

Reaman, Elmore G., *Trail of the Black Walnut*. Toronto: McClelland & Stewart, 1957, reprint 1979.

Robertson's *Landmarks of Toronto, A Collection of Historical Sketches of the Old Town of York from 1792-1833 and of Toronto from 1834-1914, Vol 1-6*. Toronto: John Ross Robertson, c1894-1914. Reprint Vol 1 & 3 Belleville: Mika Publishing, 1976 and 1974.

Rollason, Bryan, *County of a Thousand Lakes, The History of the County of Frontenac 1673-1973*. Kingston: Frontenac County Council, 1983.

Scott, James, *The Settlement of Huron County*. Toronto: Ryerson Press, 1966.

Speers, Jan, and Margaret Williams, *People of Halton: Indexes to Genealogical Sources in Halton*. Oakville: Halton Peel Branch OGS, 1983.

Wanamaker, Loral and Mildred, *Abstracts of Surrogate Court Wills, Kingston and Vicinity, 1790-1858*. Kingston Branch OGS, 1982.

Warrilow, Betty, *Tracing Your Ancestors in Bruce and Grey*. Port Elgin: Bruce and Grey Branch OGS, 1982.

Yeager, William R., *Searching For Your Ancestors in Norfolk County*. Simcoe: Norfolk Historical Society, 1976.

_____, *Wills of the London District 1800-1839*. Simcoe: Norfolk Historical Society, 1979.

Appendix III: 1842 Census Returns: Extant Townships

This Appendix is included because 1842 was the first occurrence of a wide-scale census in Ontario. Townships are listed according to the *Index of Census Returns (Ontario)*. Some townships may not be currently in the particular County as listed here. A county or township not listed did not have surviving nominal returns if any were made at the time; it might also mean that no census was taken of that township. Not necessarily all pages are extant for each return. Remember that these returns show *head of household* only.

District	County	Township
Eastern	Stormont	—
	Dundas	—
	Glengarry	—
Ottawa	Prescott	—
	Russell	—
Johnstown	Grenville	Augusta, S. Gower, Wolford,
	Leeds	Yonge, front & rear Leeds & Lansdowne, Kitley, Elizabethtown, S & N Crosby, Bastard
Victoria	Hastings	—
Bathurst	Carleton	Goulbourn, Nepean, Huntley, Fitzroy, Torbolton
	Lanark	Beckwith, Bathurst, Dalhousie, Darling, Drummond, Lanark, Lavant, Pakenham, N & S Sherbrooke
	Renfrew	Horton, Westmeath, Ross, McNab
Prince Edward	Prince Edward	—
Midland	Frontenac	Kingston Ward 4
	Lennox	—
	Addington	—
Newcastle	Northumberland	Hamilton, Haldimand, Cramahe, Murray, Seymour, Percy, Monaghan
	Durham	Clarke, Darlington, Manvers, Cartwright
Home	York	All Home District returns are aggregate,
	Simcoe	no names, except the 5 wards for City
	Ontario	of Toronto
Niagara	Lincoln	Clinton, Gainsborough
	Welland	Niagara (Town), Niagara, Stamford, Thorold, Wainfleet, Willoughby
	Haldimand	Canborough, Cayuga, Rainham, Walpole
Gore	Peel	—
	Halton	Trafalgar, Esquesing
	Wentworth	Hamilton City, Barton
	Brant	Brantford Indian Reserve
Wellington	Wellington	—
	Waterloo	—
Brock	Oxford	—
Talbot	Norfolk	—
London	Middlesex	Adelaide, Caradoc, Delaware, N Dorchester, Ekfrid, Lobo, Mosa, Westminster, London (Town), London,
	Elgin	Aldborough, Dunwich, Southwold, Yarmouth, Malahide, Bayham, S Dorchester

(cont'd p. 63)

Some column headings on the 1842 census.
(Courtesy Ontario Genealogical Society)

(cont'd from p. 61)

Western	Lambton	—
	Kent	—
	Essex	—
Huron	Huron	Ashfield, Wawanosh
	Perth	—

Appendix IV: Branches of the Ontario Genealogical Society

OGS, Brant County Branch	Box 2181, Brantford, Ont. N3T 5Y6
OGS, Bruce & Grey Branch	Box 1606, Port Elgin, Ont. N0H 2C0
OGS, Elgin County Branch	Box 416, St. Thomas, Ont. N5P 3V2
OGS, Essex County Branch	Box 2 Station A, Windsor, Ont. N9A 6J5
OGS, Halton-Peel Branch	Box 373, Oakville, Ont. L6J 5A8
OGS, Hamilton Branch	Box 904, Hamilton, Ont. L8N 3P6
OGS, Huron County Branch	R.R. 2, Clinton, Ont. N0M 1L0
OGS, Kawartha Branch	Box 162, Peterborough, Ont. K9J 6Y8
OGS, Kent County Branch	Box 964, Chatham, Ont. N7M 5L3
OGS, Kingston Branch	Box 1394, Kingston, Ont. K7L 5C6
OGS, Leeds & Grenville Branch	Box 536, Brockville, Ont. K6V 5V7
OGS, London Branch	Box 871 Station B, London, Ont. N6A 4Z3
OGS, Niagara Peninsula Branch	Box 2224 Station B, St. Catharines, Ont. L2M 6P6
OGS, Nipissing District Branch	Box 93, North Bay, Ont. P1B 8G8
OGS, Ottawa Branch	Box 8346, Ottawa, Ont. K1G 3H8
OGS, Oxford County Branch	Box 1092, Woodstock, Ont. N4S 8P6
OGS, Perth County Branch	c/o Stratford Perth Archives, 24 St. Andrew St., Stratford, Ont. N5A 1A3
OGS, Quinte Branch	Box 301, Bloomfield, Ont. K0K 1G0
OGS, Sault Ste. Marie & District Branch	Box 1203, Sault Ste Marie, Ont. P6A 6N1
OGS, Simcoe County Branch	Box 892, Barrie, Ont. L4M 4Y6
OGS, Sudbury District Branch	c/o Sudbury Public Library, 200 Brady St., Sudbury, Ont. P3E 5K3
OGS, Thunder Bay District Branch	Box 373 Station F, Thunder Bay, Ont. P7C 4V9
OGS, Toronto Branch	Box 74 Station U, Toronto, Ont. M8Z 5M4
OGS, Waterloo-Wellington Branch	Box 603, Kitchener, Ont. N2G 4A2
OGS, Whitby-Oshawa Branch	Box 174, Whitby, Ont. L1N 5S1

MAIN OFFICE
Ontario Genealogical Society
Box 66, Station Q
Toronto, Ontario, Canada
M4T 2L7